The New Wave

Critical landmarks selected by
Peter Graham

Doubleday & Company Inc.
Garden City, New York
1968

The Cinema World Series is published by
Doubleday & Company Inc.
in association with *Sight and Sound*
and the Education Department of the
British Film Institute

General Editors
Penelope Houston and Tom Milne (*Sight and Sound*)
Peter Wollen (Education Department)

First United States Publication 1968
Library of Congress Catalog Card Number: 68–23753

Designed by Farrell/Wade

Printed in Great Britain

Contents

Cover: La Mariée Était En Noir

PUBLISHERS' NOTE

We should like to thank the editors of *Cahiers du Cinéma* and *Positif* for permitting us to translate and reproduce our translation of the articles in this book; for permission to reproduce the article 'Evolution of Film Language', from André Bazin's *Qu'est-ce que le Cinéma?*, we should like to thank the University of California Press who are the holders of the English language rights of Bazin's book, and have recently published a selection of essays from it, translated by Hugh Gray, under the title *What is Cinema?*

Stills are by courtesy of Contemporary, Gala, Compton/Cameo, Rank, United Artists in France (for the cover), Connoisseur, Columbia, Twentieth Century Fox, Film Traders, Miracle Films, Paramount, and Regal.

Almost exactly ten years ago, the Nouvelle Vague burst on to the French film scene. Like the British Angry Young Man movement it was less a movement than a useful journalistic catchphrase; under it, a very heterogeneous bunch of film-makers were lumped together, some of them readily, but most of them willy-nilly.

But the Nouvelle Vague did have a nucleus of new directors who shared common cinematic ideals and who had the advantage of being both articulate and in control of a mouthpiece that had a certain prestige: Cahiers du Cinéma. *François Truffaut, Jean-Luc Godard, Claude Chabrol, Jacques Rivette, Eric Rohmer, and Jacques Doniol-Valcroze all made their first features in 1958–59, and, naturally enough, one has the impression when reading the austere, august pages of* Cahiers *of that period that they* were *the Nouvelle Vague. This transition, en bloc, and within the space of a year, of a group of men from criticism (or, if you like, theory – for their criticism was always theoretical) to creation must be unparalleled in the history of the cinema and perhaps all other arts.*

Most of the films of the Cahiers *directors are well known to British filmgoers. The publication of* Cahiers du Cinéma in English *now makes their writing available too. But its place in contemporary French criticism and culture may be less familiar. One of the aims of this book is to fill in some of the gaps: to trace the origins of their aesthetics, to indicate the enormous influence of the late André Bazin, to give examples of the sort of criticism they were writing before they became*

7

directors, and to suggest some of the problems of transition.

But I hope also to give a fairer and more representative picture of the currents of French film criticism than the one to be obtained from the pages of Cahiers. *It has often been assumed, and understandably so because of the Nouvelle Vague, that* Cahiers *represents the* only *important school of criticism. There are, of course, several other good film magazines in France (such as* Cinéma 68, *for example). But the only one which could be said to form a school, and a school diametrically opposed to that of* Cahiers, *is* Positif. *The critics of* Positif *were not lucky, or adroit, enough to cash in on the Nouvelle Vague phenomenon and pass, as many of them would have liked to have done, from criticism to direction. But they none the less represent a wide section of critical opinion. And so a couple of their most important articles on the Nouvelle Vague have been included as a foil to the other pieces.*

But the phenomenon of the Nouvelle Vague was not purely a question of cinematic ideology. It was above all a revolution in production, *in the attitude of the public and, in particular, producers. If it allowed the* Cahiers *group, like skilful surf-riders, to sweep along just ahead of the crest of the wave and give the impression of drawing along with them other new directors, the facts of the situation were that experienced makers of shorts, such as Alain Resnais and Georges Franju, had the chance to make their first features; and it became much easier for young film-makers such as Alexandre Astruc, Roger Vadim, and Louis Malle, who had already made one feature, to go on to make others.*

What was the kind of atmosphere prevalent at the time? Truffaut, looking back on that period, describes it well:

1: Interview with François Truffaut

Where, in your opinion, does the Nouvelle Vague stand today?

It varies from day to day. At the moment, things are not looking as rosy as all that. But one should not forget that when things were going well, our wildest hopes were surpassed. At the end of 1959, there was a kind of euphoric ease in production that would have been unthinkable a couple of years earlier. I remember, for instance, an article by Marguerite Duras in which she described working on *Hiroshima, Mon Amour* with Resnais. Resnais told her that they would have to work on the principle that it would be a wonderful thing if they could manage to get the film a commercial release. Compared with these modest intentions at the start, the international success of *Hiroshima* is, I think, very significant.

We all had roughly the same experience. When I was shooting *Les Quatre Cents Coups* I was horrified to see that my budget – about £20,000 – had gone up to £25,000. I got into a panic, and felt I had involved myself in something that would not easily make a profit. But once it was finished, the film more than paid for itself, what with the Cannes Film Festival and sales abroad. In the USA alone, it was bought for £35,000.

Certain producers believed the secret to success lay solely in youth, novelty, and so on; and they lost no time in prospecting for new talent. One thing is perhaps worth remembering: the first failures were the result of compromises. Say a producer was launching a director who had never made a film before. He would say to himself: all he needs is a first-class lighting cameraman. Well, it can be a very great mistake to give a beginner a cameraman whose style is classical. The end-product will be a formless hybrid. Such cameramen cannot help young directors in the way that, say, Decae or Coutard can. What's more, they cannot make a director turn out a classical, traditionally made film either.

People made the same mistake in other ways, by imposing traditional scriptwriters or stars on films that were not suitable for them. We too were led astray by erroneous ideas about how we ought to approach the cinema. When we began to want to make films, Rivette was the most active among us. At that time, only Astruc could really consider himself a film director. And whereas the rest of us just thought about the cinema without quite daring to formulate our ideas, Rivette was the first to propose a concrete solution. He made us get together, he put forward suggestions such as the idea of associated film-makers, of groups of directors, and other similar ideas. I remember we approached Resnais, and asked him if he was interested in participating in our group. On paper, it looked wonderfully simple: Astruc would make a film with Resnais as assistant, Resnais would make a film with Rivette as assistant, Rivette would make a film with myself as assistant, and so on with Bitsch and Chabrol. We discussed the budget – and we went into it quite thoroughly – and saw that we could make each film comfortably for £18,000. We then had the further idea of approaching such and such a producer, and saying: 'You make a film for £75,000 without knowing whether you'll get your money back or not. We'll make you four films for the same price, and one of them is damn well bound to be a success.'

Resnais was interested, so was Astruc, but he was already a professional, with thousands of appointments and heaps of fat scenarios lying around. So we went to see people like Dorfmann and Bérard, with a script that had been written by Rivette, Chabrol, Bitsch, and myself, and which Rivette was to direct, called *Les Quatre Jeudis*. It was a script which was based on a real event and was greatly influenced by the American cinema (of the Ray school).

I think the film would have had the same qualities and defects as a film like Alain Cavalier's *Le Combat Dans L'Ile*. It would have been torn between French realism and American schematisation. As far as I can remember, Roger Leenhardt made some pretty tough but justified criticisms of it. Anyway, we submitted the script, but no one was enthusiastic about it and that was the end of that.

It turned out that we were mistaken in thinking that producers were interested in producing low budget films. We did not know the old rule of French cinema, whereby the producer is not the man with the money but the one who finds it, and that his only certain profit comes from his percentage on the film's budget, which itself includes his salary on the one side, and the cost of the film plus unforeseen expenses on the other. The higher the budget of the film, the higher his percentage. That's why people make films for £200,000 and more when they could cost half as much, and why the last thing they care about is how the film does at the box-office. Of course, to a certain extent they *do* care about this, but as far as big budget films are concerned, whatever happens they end up with a fair salary – which makes them practically speaking employees.

That's why it did not work. The author of the film would also have to be its producer, so that the interests involved in the film affected one and the same person, instead of conflicting.

It's commonly said that the present crisis is a crisis of young directors.

True, but old directors are also affected. And the Nouvelle Vague is certainly not finished. The two most Nouvelle Vague producers in Paris, Braunberger and Beauregard, are still in business, whereas there are rumours that Jean-Paul Guibert, the producer of all Gabin's films, is losing heart. When Guibert loses £100,000 or more on *Le Bateau d'Emile*, it's the equivalent of what Beauregard will lose on three or four of his films which have not done well. What's unfair is that one never sees articles in the national Press about the failure of certain films such as *Le Président*, *Le Bateau d'Emile*, or *Un Singe en Hiver*. Far from it. A careful publicity campaign gives the impression that they are successes. The same was true of *La Fayette*, which was one of the biggest disasters of

New Wave directors at a meeting organised by Unifrance Film at the Cannes Film Festival. From left to right (*front row*), François Truffaut, Raymond Vogel, Louis Felix, Edmond Séchan; (*second row*), Edouard Molinaro, Jacques Baratier, Jean Valère; (*third row*), François Reichenbach, Robert Hossein, Jean-Daniel Pollet, Roger Vadim, Marcel Camus; (*back row*), Claude Chabrol, Jacques Doniol-Valcroze, Jean-Luc Godard, Jacques Rozier →

recent years. It lost almost half a million pounds, about half its total budget.

Doesn't this mean that the public has changed?

Why did *Le Bateau d'Emile* fail when, in spite of a high budget, it seemed pretty certain of breaking even? Because the film offers the public nothing it cannot see on television. It's a realistic film in the French tradition. The snag is that there are two or three programmes a week on television which are of exactly the same type. And although the actors in them are not well-known stars, they do hold their public.

Roughly speaking, in a large French town of 200,000 or 300,000 inhabitants there are some 15,000 students. When *Vivre Sa Vie* is showing at a cinema, they go to see it. The critics have been enthusiastic about it, and this naturally intrigues them. At least 10,000 of them take the trouble to go and see it. That is far more than can be bothered to go and see *Le Bateau d'Emile*. There's hope for us here.

Isn't the system of distribution badly organised? It was designed for films that are now out of date.

That's true. But I'm temperamentally opposed to any kind of discrimination, and would not like to see the creation of a cinema circuit specialising in Nouvelle Vague films, parallel to a larger more general circuit. I don't think a film should address a limited audience; this seems to me to contradict its function. We are in show business, and all films should have the same distribution. This of course does not mean that the cinema manager should not use his head. If people are used to seeing Westerns and he suddenly puts on *Lola*, obviously wavelengths are going to get muddled up and all three – the manager, the public, and the film – will suffer. Ideally, of course, people who go to see Westerns should also go to see *Lola*, and vice versa, but this certainly would not be the best way to go about it.

Similarly, the distributor should know certain things which unfortunately he does not. If it so happens that the distributor can be almost certain that his film is going to be torn to pieces by the critics, he is perhaps better advised to release it in the provinces first; whereas if it looks as though the critics will be favourable, Paris should get the first look.

The vituperative, fearless, and much-feared Truffaut who used to demolish films by the dozen when he was a critic on Arts *in the 1950s might have been a trifle surprised to find himself getting down so expertly to the brass tacks of distribution, entries, budgets, etc. in 1962. But he explains his change of attitude later on in the same interview: having now made films himself, it is impossible for him to retain the detached and abstract attitude necessary for a total condemnation of a film, or for a total disregard of financial considerations.*

But let's go back to the origins of the Cahiers *approach. One of the first important statements – it might even be called a manifesto – concerning a new approach to film-making was Astruc's now legendary article 'The Birth of a New Avant-Garde: La Caméra-Stylo'. Parts of it may seem tame or obvious to us today, but at the time it was written (1948) and in context of almost all the film criticism of the day, it was a veritable call for a revolution.*

2: The birth of a new avant-garde: La caméra-stylo

Alexandre Astruc

'What interests me in the cinema is abstraction.' (Orson Welles)

One cannot help noticing that something is happening in the cinema at the moment. Our sensibilities have been in danger of getting blunted by those everyday films which, year in year out, show their tired and conventional faces to the world.

The cinema of today is getting a new face. How can one tell? Simply by using one's eyes. Only a film critic could fail to notice the striking facial transformation which is taking place before our very eyes. In which films can this new beauty be found? Precisely those which have been ignored by the critics. It is not just a coincidence that Renoir's *La Règle du Jeu*, Welles's films, and Bresson's *Les Dames du Bois de Boulogne*, all films which establish the foundations of a new future for the cinema, have escaped the attention of critics, who in any case were not capable of spotting them.

But it is significant that the films which fail to obtain the blessing of the critics are precisely those which myself and several of my friends all agree about. We see in them, if you like, something of the prophetic. That's why I am talking about *avant-garde*. There is always an *avant-garde* when something new takes place. . . .

To come to the point: the cinema is quite simply becoming a means of expression, just as all the other arts have been before it, and in particular painting and the novel. After having been successively a fairground attraction, an amusement analogous to boulevard

Alexandre Astruc

La Règle du Jeu

theatre, or a means of preserving the images of an era, it is gradually becoming a language. By language, I mean a form in which and by which an artist can express his thoughts, however abstract they may be, or translate his obsessions exactly as he does in the contemporary essay or novel. That is why I would like to call this new age of cinema the age of *caméra-stylo* (camera-pen). This metaphor has a very precise sense. By it I mean that the cinema will gradually break free from the tyranny of what is visual, from the image for its own sake, from the immediate and concrete demands of the narrative, to become a means of writing just as flexible and subtle as written language. This art, although blessed with an enormous potential, is an easy prey to prejudice; it cannot go on for ever ploughing the same field of realism and social fantasy* which has been bequeathed to it by the popular novel. It can tackle any sub-

---

*Carné liked to use these terms when referring to his pre-war films (Ed.).

ject, any genre. The most philosophical meditations on human production, psychology, metaphysics, ideas, and passions lie well within its province. I will even go so far as to say that contemporary ideas and philosophies of life are such that only the cinema can do justice to them. Maurice Nadeau wrote in an article in the newspaper *Combat*: 'If Descartes lived today, he would write novels.' With all due respect to Nadeau, a Descartes of today would already have shut himself up in his bedroom with a 16mm camera and some film, and would be writing his philosophy on film: for his *Discours de la Méthode* would today be of such a kind that only the cinema could express it satisfactorily.

It must be understood that up to now the cinema has been nothing more than a show. This is due to the basic fact that all films are projected in an auditorium. But with the development of 16mm and television, the day is not far off when everyone will possess a projector, will go to the local bookstore and hire films written on any subject, of any form, from literary criticism and novels to mathematics, history, and general science. From that moment on, it will no longer be possible to speak of *the* cinema. There will be *several* cinemas just as today there are several literatures, for the cinema, like literature, is not so much a particular art as a language which can express any sphere of thought.

This idea of the cinema expressing ideas is not perhaps a new one. Feyder has said: 'I could make a film with Montesquieu's *L'Esprit des Lois*.' But Feyder was thinking of illustrating it 'with pictures' just as Eisenstein had thought of illustrating Marx's *Capital* in book fashion. What I am trying to say is that the cinema is now moving towards a form which is making it such a precise language that it will soon be possible to write ideas directly on film without even having to resort to those heavy associations of images that were the delight of the silent cinema. In other words, in order to suggest the passing of time, there is no need to show falling leaves and then apple trees in blossom; and in order to suggest that a hero wants to make love there are surely other ways of going about it than showing a saucepan of milk boiling over on to the stove, as Clouzot does in *Quai des Orfèvres*.

The fundamental problem of the cinema is how to express thought. The creation of this language has preoccupied all the theoreticians and writers in the history of the cinema, from Eisenstein down to the scriptwriters and adaptors of the sound cinema. But neither the silent cinema, because it was the slave of a static conception of the image, nor the classical sound cinema, as it has existed right up to now, has been able to solve this problem satisfactorily. The silent cinema thought it could get out of it through editing and the juxtaposition of images. Remember Eisenstein's famous statement: 'Editing is for me the means of giving movement (i.e. an idea) to two static images.' And when sound came, he was content to adapt theatrical devices.

One of the fundamental phenomena of the last few years has been the growing realisation of the dynamic, i.e. significant, character of the cinematic image. Every film, because its primary function is to move, i.e. to take place in time, is a theorem. It is a series of images which, from one end to the other, have an inexorable logic (or better even, a dialectic) of their own. We have come to realise that the meaning which the silent cinema tried to give birth to through symbolic association exists within the image itself, in the development of the narrative, in every gesture of the characters, in every line of dialogue, in those camera movements which relate objects to objects and characters to objects. All thought, like all feeling, is a relationship between one human being and another human being or certain objects which form part of his universe. It is by clarifying these relationships, by making a tangible allusion, that the cinema can really make itself the vehicle of thought. From today onwards, it will be possible for the cinema to produce works which are equivalent, in their profundity and meaning, to the novels of Faulkner and Malraux, to the essays of Sartre and Camus. Moreover we already have a significant example: Malraux's *L'Espoir*, the film which he directed from his own novel, in which, perhaps for the first time ever, film language is the exact equivalent of literary language.

Let us now have a look at the way people make concessions to the supposed (but fallacious) requirements of the cinema. Script-

Malraux's *L'Espoir*

writers who adapt Balzac or Dostoievsky excuse the idiotic trans-
formations they impose on the works from which they construct
their scenarios by pleading that the cinema is incapable of rendering
every psychological or metaphysical overtone. In their hands,
Balzac becomes a collection of engravings in which fashion has the
most important place, and Dostoievsky suddenly begins to resemble
the novels of Joseph Kessel, with Russian-style drinking-bouts in
night-clubs and troika races in the snow. Well, the only cause of
these compressions is laziness and lack of imagination. The cinema
of today is capable of expressing any kind of reality. What interests
us is the creation of this new language. We have no desire to rehash
those poetic documentaries and surrealist films of twenty-five years
ago every time we manage to escape the demands of a commercial
industry. Let's face it: between the pure cinema of the 1920s and
filmed theatre, there is plenty of room for a different and individual
kind of film-making.

This of course implies that the scriptwriter directs his own scripts; or rather, that the scriptwriter ceases to exist, for in this kind of film-making the distinction between author and director loses all meaning. Direction is no longer a means of illustrating or presenting a scene, but a true act of writing. The film-maker/author writes with his camera as a writer writes with his pen. In an art in which a length of film and sound-track is put in motion and proceeds, by means of a certain form and a certain story (there can even be no story at all – it matters little), to evolve a philosophy of life, how can one possibly distinguish between the man who conceives the work and the man who writes it ? Could one imagine a Faulkner novel written by someone other than Faulkner ? And would *Citizen Kane* be satisfactory in any other form than that given to it by Orson Welles ?

Let me say once again that I realise the term *avant-garde* savours of the surrealist and so-called abstract films of the 1920s. But that *avant-garde* is already old hat. It was trying to create a specific domain for the cinema; we on the contrary are seeking to broaden it and make it the most extensive and clearest language there is. Problems such as the translation into cinematic terms of verbal tenses and logical relationships interest us much more than the creation of the exclusively visual and static art dreamt of by the surrealists. In any case, they were doing no more than make cinematic adaptations of their experiments in painting and poetry.

So there we are. This has nothing to do with a school, or even a movement. Perhaps it could simply be called a tendency: a new awareness, a desire to transform the cinema and hasten the advent of an exciting future. Of course, no tendency can be so called unless it has something concrete to show for itself. The films will come, they will see the light of day – make no mistake about it. The economic and material difficulties of the cinema create the strange paradox whereby one can talk about something which does not yet exist; for although we know what we want, we do not know whether, when, and how we will be able to do it. But the cinema cannot but develop. It is an art that cannot live by looking back over the past and chewing over the nostalgic memories of an age gone by. Already it is looking to the future; for the future, in the cinema as elsewhere, is the only thing that matters.

Astruc's call for a totally independent means of expression is one that no one, of whatever school, would take exception to. The champions of 'specificity' were later to twist his argument to fit their own pet theory that a film can be judged only in so far as it is specific, or differs from the other arts, i.e. visually. But Astruc's own films confirmed what he had said in this article: he conceived of a total *cinema in which every component part, whether already existing in the arts, like words and music, or new and specific to the cinema, like visual and spatial movement, should have equal importance.*

Much more directly influential than Astruc, though his theories too were later traduced by his disciples, was André Bazin. In 1947 he founded La Revue du Cinéma, *which became* Cahiers du Cinéma *in 1950. He remained one of its editors and its spiritual leader until his death at the age of forty in 1958. A convinced Catholic, he wrote a large number of cogent articles or studies, on such varied subjects as eroticism in the cinema, filmed theatre, neo-realism, the Western, and the myth of Stalin in the Soviet cinema. But the article of his which probably had the greatest influence over the thinking of the* Cahiers *directors was 'The evolution of film language'.*

3: The evolution of film language

André Bazin

By 1928, the art of the silent film was at its height. Many of the best directors were understandably, though not justifiably, sorry to witness the disappearance of this perfect world of images. They felt that the cinema, having taken a certain aesthetic direction, had become an art that was supremely suited to what was known as the 'exquisite unnaturalness' of silence. The realism of sound was bound to upset matters.

In fact, now that the use of sound has satisfactorily proved that far from annihilating the Old Testament of the cinema it has brought it to fulfilment, one might well ask oneself if the technical revolution that resulted from the introduction of sound could really be called an aesthetic revolution. In other words, did the years 1928–30 really witness the birth of a new cinema? As far as the way a film is put together is concerned, the history of the cinema does not in fact reveal as marked a difference as one might expect between the silent and sound cinema. There are many affinities to be found between certain directors of the twenties and others of the thirties and especially the forties – between, for instance, Erich von Stroheim and Jean Renoir or Orson Welles, Carl Theodor Dreyer and Robert Bresson. These more or less marked affinities prove first of all that the dividing line of 1930 was no barrier, that certain qualities of the silent cinema were carried over into the sound era, but above all that instead of contrasting 'sound' with 'silent' films we should examine in what way they differed from *and* resembled each other in conception and style.

I am quite aware that the brevity of this essay will oblige me to make some critical simplifications, and I shall regard what I put forward more as a working hypothesis than an objective truth. With this in mind, I would say that by and large there were two opposing schools in the cinema from 1920 to 1940: directors who believed in the image and those who believed in reality.

By 'image', I mean in a general sense anything that can be added to a depicted object by its being depicted on the screen. This addition is complex, but it can be traced back to two factors: the plasticity of the image and the resources of editing (in other words, the organisation of images in time). By plasticity I mean the style of the sets and the make-up, to a certain extent even the acting, and of course the lighting and framing which complete the composition. As for the editing, which, as is well known, had its source in Griffith's masterpieces, André Malraux wrote in *The Psychology of the Cinema* that it constitutes the birth of the film as an art: editing is what truly distinguishes it from simple animated photography and makes it a language.

The use of editing can be 'invisible'; and this was most frequently the case in the classical pre-war American film. The only purpose of breaking down the shots is to analyse an event according to the physical and dramatic logic of a scene. This analysis is rendered imperceptible by its very logicality. The spectator's mind naturally accepts the camera angles that the director offers him because they are justified by the disposition of the action or the shifting of dramatic interest.

But the neutrality of this 'invisible' breakdown of sequences does not take into account the full possibilities of editing. These are to be found in three devices generally known as 'parallel editing', 'accelerated editing', and 'editing by attraction'. In creating parallel editing, Griffith managed to evoke the simultaneity of two widely separated actions, by a succession of shots of first one, then the other. In *La Roue*, Abel Gance creates the illusion of an accelerating locomotive without having recourse to any real images of speed (for all we know, the wheels might as well be revolving on the spot), simply by an accumulation of shorter and shorter shots. Finally, editing by attraction, conceived by Eisenstein and more difficult to describe, might be broadly defined as the reinforcement of the meaning of one image by another image which does not necessarily belong to the same action: for instance, the cascade of light, in *The General Line*, which follows the shot of the bull. In this extreme form, editing by attraction has not been used very frequently, even by its originator, but the much more general practice of ellipse, comparison, or metaphor is basically very similar: for instance, stockings thrown on to the chair at the foot of the bed, or even spilt milk (in Clouzot's *Quai des Orfèvres*).

Naturally there exist various combinations of these three devices. But whatever they are, they have a common recognisable feature (which could serve as the very definition of editing): the creation of a meaning which is not contained objectively in the individual images themselves, but which arises from their collocation. Kuleshov's famous experiment with the same shot of Moszhukhin, whose smile seemed to change in implication according to the shot that preceded it, is a perfect summary of the properties of editing.

Kuleshov, Eisenstein, and Gance do not show the event through their editing; they allude to it. True, they take most of their elements from the reality they are supposed to be describing, but the final meaning of the film lies much more in the organisation of these elements than in their objective content. The substance of the narrative, whatever the realism of the individual shots, arises essentially from these relationships (Moszhukhin smiling plus dead child = pity); that is to say there is an abstract result whose origins are not to be found in any of the concrete elements. In the same way, one could imagine that young girls plus apple trees in blossom = hope. The combinations are innumerable. But they all have one thing in common: they suggest an idea by means of a metaphor or an association of ideas. And so between the scenario proper – the ultimate object of the narrative – and the raw image, a supplementary link is inserted, a kind of aesthetic 'transformer'. The meaning is not *in* the image, but is merely a shadow of it, projected by the editing on the consciousness of the spectator.

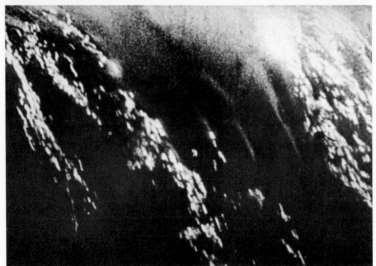

Bull and cascade in *The General Line*

To sum up: both the plastic content of the image and the possibilities of editing mean that the cinema disposes of a whole arsenal of devices with which it can impose its own interpretation of a depicted event on the spectator. By the end of the silent era, one can consider this arsenal to have been complete. The Soviet cinema took the theory and practice of editing to their ultimate conclusions, whereas the German expressionist school subjected the plasticity of the image (sets and lighting) to every possible distortion. The German and Soviet cinemas were certainly not the only important schools at the time, and one could hardly claim that in France, Sweden, or America film language lacked the means to say what it had to say. If the essence of cinematic art is to be found in all that plasticity and editing can add to a given reality, then the silent cinema was a complete art. Sound could have played only a subordinate and complementary role, as a counterpoint to the visual image. But this kind of potential enrichment (which at the best of times could only have been minor) would have paled beside the whole range of supplementary reality that was in fact introduced by sound.

What we have done is to suppose that expressionism in the editing and the image is the essential part of film art. It is precisely this generally accepted notion that is implicitly challenged, as early as the silent era, by directors such as Erich von Stroheim, F. W. Murnau, or Robert Flaherty. Editing plays practically no role at all in their films, except in the purely negative sense of eliminating what is superfluous. The camera cannot see everything at once, but at least it tries not to miss anything of what it has chosen to see. For Flaherty, the important thing to show when Nanook hunts the seal is the relationship between the man and the animal and the true proportions of Nanook's lying in wait. Editing could have suggested the passage of time; Flaherty is content to *show* the waiting, and the duration of the hunt becomes the very substance and object of the image. In the film this episode consists of a single shot. Can anyone deny that it is in this way much more moving than 'editing by attraction' would have been ?

Nanook hunts the seal

Murnau is less interested in time than in the reality of dramatic space: in neither *Nosferatu* nor *Sunrise* does editing play a decisive part. One might perhaps suppose that the plasticity of Murnau's images has an affinity with a certain kind of expressionism; but this would be a superficial view. The way Murnau composes his images is not at all pictorial, it adds nothing to reality, it does not deform it; rather it strives to bring out the deeper structure of reality, to reveal pre-existent relationships which become the constituents of the drama. Thus, in *Tabu*, the entry of a ship into the left of the screen makes the spectator see it as a metaphor of fate, without Murnau in any way distorting the strict realism of the film, shot entirely on location.

But it was without doubt Stroheim who was the most reluctant to use visual expressionism and editing devices. In his work, reality admits its meaning like a suspect who is being grilled by an indefatigable police inspector. The principle of his direction, a simple one, is to look at the world from so close and with such insistence that it ends up by revealing its cruelty and its ugliness. One can well imagine, in theory, a Stroheim film composed of a single shot, which would be as long and as close up as one liked.

I do not want to limit my case to these three directors. We shall certainly find others, here and there, who reject expressionist elements and do not rely on editing to play a large part. Even Griffith is one of them, for example. But perhaps these examples will suffice to show that in the middle of the silent period there existed a film art that was diametrically opposed to what is normally thought to be true cinema, a language whose syntactic and semantic components are not at all the individual shots: the images are important not for what they add to reality but for what they reveal in it. The silent cinema could only counteract this tendency. Both *Greed* and *La Passion de Jeanne d'Arc* are virtually sound films. Once editing and visual composition cease to be considered as the very essence of film language, it can be seen that the arrival of sound was not an aesthetic watershed dividing two radically different aspects of the medium. Some people saw that sound was bringing a certain kind of cinema to an end; but this was not at all *the* cinema. The true cleavage plane was elsewhere; it was, and still is, cutting clean across thirty-five years of the history of cinematic expression.

Now that the aesthetic unity of the silent cinema is not as solid as it seemed, caught as it is between two strongly contrasting tendencies, we should perhaps take another look at the history of the last twenty years.

From 1930 to 1940, a certain kinship of expression in the cinema grew up throughout the world, originating in particular from America. Hollywood was riding high with five or six well-tried types of film which gave it overwhelming superiority: the American comedy (*Mr Smith Goes to Washington*, 1939), the burlesque film (the Marx Brothers), the song and dance musical (Fred Astaire and Ginger Rogers, *Ziegfeld Follies*, 1945), the gangster film (*Scarface*, 1932, *I was a Fugitive from a Chain Gang*, 1932, *The Informer*, 1935), the psychological and social drama (*Back Street*, 1932, *Jezebel*, 1938), the horror film (*Dr Jekyll and Mr Hyde*, 1931, *The Invisible*

Le Jour se Lève

Man, 1933, *Frankenstein*, 1931), the Western (*Stagecoach*, 1939). During the same period, the French cinema was undoubtedly the next best after the American: its quality gradually emerged in the trend which might broadly be termed 'black realism' or 'poetic realism', and which was dominated by four directors: Jacques Feyder, Jean Renoir, Marcel Carné, and Julien Duvivier. As it is not my purpose to award prizes, there would not be much point in lingering on the Soviet, British, German, and Italian films of this period, which were relatively less important than they were to be during the following ten years. In any case, the American and French films will suffice to demonstrate clearly that the pre-war sound cinema was an art that had visibly reached well-balanced maturity.

A word about content first of all: there were the well-tried genres, governed by carefully worked-out laws, capable of entertaining the largest possible international public, and also of attracting a cultivated élite, as long as these felt no *a priori* hostility towards the cinema.

As for form, the photographic and narrative styles were perfectly clear and they conformed with their subject: a total reconciliation of sound and image. When one re-sees films like William Wyler's *Jezebel*, John Ford's *Stagecoach*, or Marcel Carné's *Le Jour se Lève* today, one senses an art that has attained a perfect balance, an ideal form of expression. Conversely, one admires dramatic and moral themes which, although not entirely creations of the cinema, were raised to a certain nobility, to an artistic effectiveness that they would not have achieved without it. In short, these were all characteristics of 'classic' art in full flower.

I am perfectly aware that there is a case for maintaining that the originality of the post-war cinema, compared with that of 1939, lies in the emergence of certain individual countries as film-producers, especially in the dazzling explosion of the Italian cinema and the appearance of a British cinema that was original and free from influences from Hollywood; that the truly important phenomenon of the forties was the infusion of new blood, the opening up of unexplored regions; that the real revolution took place more on the level of subject-matter than of style, and concerned what the cinema had to say to the world rather than the way of saying it. Is not neo-realism above all a kind of humanism rather than a style of direction? And is not the essential feature of this style self-effacement before reality?

It is certainly not my intention to champion some supposed superiority of form over content. 'Art for art's sake' is just as heretical in the cinema as it is elsewhere, perhaps even more so! But new wine should not be put into old bottles! And one way of understanding better what a film is trying to say is to know how it is saying it.

In 1938 or 1939, then, the sound cinema had, especially in France and America, reached a degree of classical perfection that was based both on the maturity of the dramatic genres that had been developed over ten years or inherited from the silent cinema, and on the stabilisation of technical progress. The thirties saw the arrival of panchromatic film as well as sound. Of course, the studios never stopped trying to improve their equipment, but these improvements were only incidental – none of them opened up radically new possibilities in film direction. Moreover this situation has not changed since 1940, except possibly in the field of photography, thanks to an increase in the sensitivity of film. Panchromatic film upset the balance of values in the image, and ultra-sensitive emulsions allowed modifications to be made in the composition. Now that the director of photography was free to shoot in a studio with a much smaller lens aperture, he could, if necessary, eliminate the blurred backgrounds that used to be the rule. But one can find plenty of examples of depth of focus being employed well before then (by Jean Renoir, for instance); it had always been possible in exteriors and even in the studio with a little ingenuity. It was there to be resorted to if the director so desired. And so what is important here is not so much the technical problem, although the solution of this was considerably facilitated, as the stylistic effect (which I will come back to). In short, ever since the use of panchromatic film and the possibilities offered by the microphone and the crane became general in studios, the technical conditions necessary and sufficient for the creation of film art had been achieved by 1930.

As technical requirements played practically no part in this, the signs and the principles of the evolution in language must be sought elsewhere: in the renewal of subject-matter and, in consequence, of the styles that were needed to express it. In 1939, the sound cinema had reached a point which geographers call the line of equilibrium of a river, i.e. that ideal mathematical curve that is the result of sufficient erosion. Once a river attains its line of equilibrium, it flows effortlessly from its source to its mouth without hollowing out its bed further. But if any geological shift occurs which raises the peneplain or alters the altitude of the source, the water becomes active again, penetrating the underlying land, sinking in, undermining, and hollowing out. Occasionally, if there is a bed of limestone, a whole new network of hollows forms on the plateau; it is scarcely perceptible, but is complex and contorted if one follows the way the water takes.

In 1938, the way shots were broken down in a shooting script was the same almost everywhere. If, to be conventional, we call the type of silent film based on visual and editing devices 'expressionist' or 'symbolic', we might dub the new form of narrative 'analytic' and 'dramatic'. Suppose, to go back to one of the elements in Kuleshov's experiment, we have a table laden with food and a poor famished beggar. In 1936, the breakdown might have been as follows:

1. General shot taking in both the actor and the table.
2. Tracking shot forward ending in a close-up of his face which expresses a mixture of wonder and desire.
3. A series of close-ups of the food.
4. Back to the character (in medium shot) who walks slowly towards the camera.
5. Slight track back to take in the actor from the knees up, seizing a chicken's wing.

There could be many variations on this breakdown, but they would all still have several things in common:

1. Spatial verisimilitude, whereby the position of the character is always determined, even when a close-up cuts out the décor.
2. The intention and effect of this breakdown are exclusively dramatic or psychological.

In other words, if this scene were acted on stage and seen from a seat in the stalls, it would have exactly the same meaning; the event would still have an objective existence. The change in camera angles does not add anything, it simply presents reality in the most effective manner. First of all by allowing one to see it better, and then by emphasising what needs emphasising.

True, the film director, just like the theatre producer, has a margin of interpretation within which he can inflect the meaning of the action. But this is only a margin, and it cannot modify the formal logic of what takes place. By way of contrast, take the editing of the stone lions in *Battleship Potemkin*; skilfully put together, a series of shots of different pieces of sculpture give the impression that one lion (like the people) is getting to its feet. This admirable

The stone lions in *Battleship Potemkin*

editing device was unthinkable after 1932. In *Fury*, Fritz Lang inserted, as late as 1935, a shot of clucking chickens in a farmyard after a series of shots of tittle-tattling women. This was a survival from the age of editing by attraction which brought people up in their seats even at the time and now seems totally out of place in the context of the rest of the film. However marked the art of a director like Carné may be, for instance in his enhancement of the scenarios of *Quai des Brumes* and *Le Jour se Lève*, his breakdown of shots remains on the same level as the events it is analysing. It is just a good way of looking at them. This is why we are witnessing the almost complete disappearance of special visual effects, such as superimposition, and even, especially in America, the close-up, which has such a violent physical effect that it makes one aware the director has cut from one shot to another. In the typical American comedy, the director returns as often as he can to a shot of the

characters from the knees up (the so-called *plan américain*), which accords best with the spontaneous attentiveness of the spectator – it is a point of natural equilibrium for his mental accommodation.

In fact, this use of editing has its origins in the silent cinema. This is more or less the part it plays in Griffith's work, in *Broken Blossoms* for example; but with *Intolerance*, Griffith was already beginning to introduce the synthetic conception of editing which the Soviet cinema was to take to its ultimate conclusions and which can be found, less exclusively, in several films at the end of the silent period. Besides, it is understandable that the sound image, being much less malleable than the visual image, made editing more realistic again and to an ever-increasing extent eliminated both plastic expressionism and symbolic relationships between images.

And so in about 1938, films were almost always put together according to the same principles. The story was told by a succession of shots, which varied very little in number (around six hundred per film). The characteristic technique of this type of narrative was cross-cutting, which, in a dialogue for instance, consists of alternate shots of either speaker according to the logic of the text. This type of shooting script, which perfectly suited the best films of 1930–39, was strongly challenged by the technique of composition in depth used by Orson Welles and William Wyler.

The reputation of *Citizen Kane* is no exaggeration. Thanks to composition in depth, whole scenes are filmed in a single shot (a device known as the sequence-shot), sometimes even without the camera moving. The dramatic effects which used to depend on the editing are all obtained here by the movements of the actors within a chosen framing. Welles did not of course 'invent' composition in depth, any more than Griffith did the close-up; all the early pioneers of the cinema used it, and with good reason. The partially blurred image, which came in only with editing, was not simply due to technical subservience resulting from the use of close shots; it was the logical consequence of editing, its plastic equivalent. If at a certain point in the action the director takes for example, as in the imaginary sequence already mentioned, a close-up of a fruit-bowl, it is normal for him also to isolate it in space by the focusing of the lens. A blurred background confirms an editing effect. Whereas it is only an accessory part of the style of photography, it is an essential part of the style of the narrative. Jean Renoir understood this perfectly when he wrote in 1938, i.e. after *La Bête Humaine* and *La Grande Illusion* and before *La Règle du Jeu*: 'The longer I work in my profession, the more I am drawn to *mise-en-scène* in depth in relation to the screen; the more I do that, the more I am able to avoid the confrontation of two actors who stand like good boys in front of the camera as though they were at the photographer's.' And in fact if one looks for a precursor to Orson Welles, it is not Louis Lumière or Zecca but Jean Renoir. In Renoir's work, the tendency to compose the image in depth goes hand in hand with a partial suppression of editing, which is replaced by frequent panning shots and entries into frame. It implies a respect for the continuity of dramatic space and also, of course, for its duration.

Anyone who can use his eyes must realise that Welles's sequence-shots in *The Magnificent Ambersons* are by no means the passive 'recording' of an action photographed within a single frame, but that on the contrary this reluctance to break up an event or analyse its dramatic reverberations within time is a positive technique which produces better results than a classical breakdown of shots could ever have done.

One needs only to compare two stills which are composed in depth, one from a film of 1910, the other from a film by Welles or Wyler, and one will see just from looking at each still, detached from the film, that their functions are diametrically opposed. The 1910 framing more or less takes up the position of the absent fourth wall of a theatre stage or, out of doors anyway, of the best viewpoint of the action, whereas the sets, the camera angle, and the lighting in the second composition have to be looked at with different eyes. Over the surface of the screen, the director and the director of photography have managed to organise a dramatic chessboard from which no detail is excluded. The most obvious, if not the most original, examples of this are to be found in *The Little Foxes*, where the *mise-en-scène* has the precision of a blueprint (with Welles, the baroque overtones make analysis more complicated). The placing of objects in relation to the characters is such that their meaning *cannot* escape the spectator, a meaning which editing would have built up in a series of successive shots.

Take, for instance, a dramatic construction pivoted on three characters in Wyler's *The Best Years of Our Lives* (the scene where Dana Andrews and Teresa Wright break off their engagement). The sequence takes place in a bar. Fredric March has just persuaded his friend to break off with his daughter and urges him to go and telephone her immediately. Dana Andrews gets up and goes towards the call box which is by the door at the far end of the room. Fredric March puts his elbows on the piano in the foreground and pretends to be engrossed in the musical exercises of the disabled sergeant who is learning to play with the hooks he has instead of hands. The frame contains the keyboard in close shot, takes in Fredric March in close medium shot, includes the whole room, and leaves Dana Andrews quite visible, though small, right at the back in the call box. This shot is clearly governed by two points of dramatic interest and three characters. The action taking place in the foreground is of secondary importance, although interesting and unusual enough to demand our close attention, especially as it occupies a privileged position on the screen and a considerable amount of its surface. The real action, however, the one that at this point constitutes a decisive turning-point in the plot, is taking place almost secretly in a tiny rectangle at the back of the room, i.e. on the very left of the screen.

The link between these two dramatic zones is Fredric March, who is the only person, apart from the spectator, to know what is going on in the call box, and who, as is logical in such a situation, is also moved by the prowess of his disabled friend. From time to time, Fredric March turns his head slightly, and casts an anxious glance diagonally across the screen at Dana Andrews's gesticulations. The latter finally rings off and without looking round abruptly disappears into the street. If we reduce the real action to its elements, it consists basically of a telephone call made by Dana Andrews. The only thing which interests us at this moment is the telephone conversation. The only actor whose face we want to see in close-up is precisely the one whom we cannot distinguish clearly because he is so far away from the camera and behind the glass window of the call box. His words of course cannot be heard. The real drama is taking place in the distance in a kind of small aquarium which lets us see only the banal and ritual gestures of someone telephoning.

This idea of the call box at the back of the room which forces the spectator to imagine what is going on inside it, i.e. to share Fredric March's anxiety, was in itself an excellent brainwave on the part of the director. But Wyler knew very well that alone it would destroy the spatial and temporal equilibrium of the shot. It had to be both counterbalanced and reinforced. Whence the idea of a diverting action *in the foreground*, secondary in itself, but whose visual prominence would be in inverse proportion to its dramatic importance. Although a secondary action, it is not an insignificant one; the spectator is also concerned about what will happen to the disabled sergeant and so is interested in what he is doing. And anyway it is certainly not every day that one sees someone play the piano with hooks! Held in suspense and unable really to see at what point the hero finishes telephoning, the spectator is also obliged to divide his attention between the hooks and the call box. In this way, Wyler kills two birds with one stone: the diversion of the piano first of all allows him to hold for as long as necessary a shot which alone would have been interminable and inevitably monotonous, but it is above all the introduction of this pivot of subsidiary action which gives the image its dramatic organisation and quite literally its very construction. The real action is overlaid with the action of the *mise-en-scène* itself, which consists of dividing the attention of the spectator against his will, of guiding it in the right direction, and thus of making him participate in his own right in the drama created by the director.

To be more precise, I should point out that this scene is cut twice by a close shot of Fredric March looking at the call box. No doubt Wyler was afraid that the spectator would be too fascinated by the piano exercises and might gradually lose interest in the main action, i.e. the dramatic interplay between Fredric March and Dana

The sequence at the wedding in *The Best Years of Our Lives*

Andrews. The editing probably showed that the two interpolated shots were necessary to recharge the flagging attention of the audience. Such foresight is incidentally very characteristic of Wyler's technique. Orson Welles would have managed to make the call box stand out by its very remoteness and would have held the shot for as long as necessary. For Orson Welles, composition in depth is an aesthetic end in itself; for Wyler, it remains subordinate to the dramatic needs of the *mise-en-scène* and especially the clarity of the narrative. The two interpolated shots have the same effect as bold type or a heavily pencilled line.

Wyler especially likes to construct his *mise-en-scène* around the tension created in a shot by the simultaneity of two actions of disparate importance. This can be clearly seen in the still taken from the final sequence of the film.

The characters grouped on the right, in the middle ground, seem to form the main dramatic point of interest, as everyone has gathered in this room to attend the wedding of the disabled sergeant. In fact, since this action is a foregone conclusion and, in a sense, already over, the spectator's interest is focused on Teresa Wright (in white in the background) and Dana Andrews (on the left in the foreground), who are meeting for the first time since they broke off their engagement. Throughout the whole sequence of the wedding, Wyler manipulates his actors with consummate skill so as gradually to bring to the fore the two protagonists, who, the spectator is sure, are continually thinking of each other. The reproduced still shows an intermediate stage. At this point, the two centres of interest, Dana Andrews and Teresa Wright, have not yet come together, but the natural though carefully calculated movements of the other actors throw their relationship into clear relief. Teresa Wright's white dress, standing out almost in the centre of the frame, makes a kind of dramatic fissure, so that if one were to cut the image in half at the point where the walls meet the action would also be bisected into its two elements. The two lovers are visually and logically thrust into the left part of the frame.

The importance of the direction in which people look should also be noticed in this still. The look always forms the skeleton of Wyler's *mise-en-scène*. As well as the actual look of the characters, Wyler also excels at getting across to us the virtual look of the camera, with which our own eyes identify themselves. Jean Mitry has drawn attention to the low angle shot in *Jezebel* which places the lens right in line with Bette Davis's gaze as she sees the walking-stick that Henry Fonda has in his hand and intends to use. In this way we can follow the gaze of the characters better than if the camera, as in an ordinary shooting script, showed us the stick from above as if through Bette Davis's own eyes.

There is a variant of the same principles in *The Little Foxes*: in order to make us understand the thoughts of the character who notices the small steel box which used to contain some stolen shares (their absence is going to reveal his theft), Wyler puts the object in the foreground, this time with the camera at the same height as the man, but still symmetrically placed in relation to the actor and to what he is looking at. Our gaze does not meet that of

The small steel box in *The Little Foxes*

the actor directly through the regarded object, but, as through the interplay of a mirror, the angle of incidence of our own gaze on the box is somehow equivalent to the angle of reflection which leads us to the eyes of the actor. In every case, Wyler guides our mental outlook by means of the strict laws of an invisible dramatic perspective.

The spectator has only to follow the gaze of the characters like a pointing finger and he will have an exact understanding of all the intentions of the director. If these could be made tangible on the image by a pencil line, we would see, as clearly as we see the ghost of a magnet in iron filings, the dramatic forces which are crossing the screen. All Wyler's preparatory work consists of simplifying the mechanics of *mise-en-scène* as far as possible by making it as efficient and as clear as he can. In *The Best Years of Our Lives*, he attains an almost abstract purity. Every point of dramatic articulation is so sensitive that a shift of a few degrees in the angle of somebody's gaze is not only quite obvious to the most obtuse spectator, but is also capable, through a kind of leverage, of turning a whole scene upside-down.

The modern director, in using the sequence-shot with composition in depth, is not rejecting editing – how could he do so without reverting to a kind of rudimentary gibberish? He is integrating it into his visual style. The narrative of Welles and Wyler is no less explicit than that of John Ford, but it has the advantage of not having to forfeit the special effects that can be obtained from the unity of the image in time and space. It matters a great deal (at least in a work that has some style) whether an event is analysed fragment by fragment or shown in its physical unity. It would of course be absurd to deny the marked progress in film language that has been brought about by the use of editing, but it has been gained at the expense of other qualities that are no less specifically cinematic.

This is why composition in depth is not just another cameraman's device like the use of filters or of a certain type of lighting; it is a vital contribution to direction: a dialectical advance in the history of film language.

And this advance is not merely a formal one. Composition in depth, well used, is not just a more economic, subtle, and simple way of heightening an event; it affects not only the structure of film language but also the intellectual relationship between the spectator and the image, thus actually modifying the meaning of the film.

It would be beyond the scope of this article to analyse the psychological repercussions of this relationship, let alone its aesthetic consequences, but perhaps it will suffice to make the following general remarks:

1. Composition in depth means that the spectator's relationship with the image is nearer to that which he has with reality. It is then true to say that quite independently of the actual content of the image its structure is more realistic.

2. Consequently, composition in depth demands a more active mental attitude on the part of the spectator and even a positive contribution to the direction. Whereas with analytic editing he has only to follow his guide and let his attention focus on whatever the

director has chosen for him to see, a certain minimum of personal choice is required here. The fact that the image has a meaning depends partly on his attention and his will.

3. From the two preceding propositions, which are of a psychological nature, there follows a third one which might be defined as metaphysical.

By analysing reality, the very nature of editing assumes the dramatic event to have a unity of meaning. Another analytical process might be possible, but the result would be a different film. In short, the nature and essence of editing is such that it stands in the way of the expression of ambiguity. And it was precisely this that was proved by Kuleshov's *reductio ad absurdum*: each time, an exact meaning was given to the face whose ambiguity made possible these three alternately exclusive interpretations.

Composition in depth, on the other hand, brings ambiguity back into the structure of the image; this is not automatic (Wyler's films are hardly ambiguous at all), but it is certainly a possibility. That is why it is no exaggeration to say that *Citizen Kane* is conceived entirely in terms of composition in depth. One's uncertainty about the spiritual key or interpretation of the film hangs on the very composition of the image.

It is not that Welles purposely refrains from using expressionist editing techniques. In fact, their episodic use, in between sequence-shots with composition in depth, gives them new meaning. Editing had once been the very stuff of cinema, the tissue of a scenario. In *Citizen Kane*, a series of superimpositions stands in contrast to the continuity of a scene taken in a single shot; it is a different, explicitly abstract register of the narrative. Accelerated editing used to distort time and space; Welles's editing, far from attempting to deceive us, offers us a temporal résumé – the equivalent, for example, of the French imperfect tense or the English frequentative. And so 'quick editing', 'editing by attraction', and the superimpositions which the sound cinema had not resorted to for ten years, found a possible use in conjunction with the temporal realism of cinema without editing. I have dwelt on the case of Orson Welles because the date of his appearance in the cinematic firmament marks the beginning of a

Murnau's *Tabu*

new period, and also because his case is the most spectacular and significant in its very excesses. But *Citizen Kane* fits into a general movement, into a vast geological shift of strata which, in one way and another, confirms this revolution in expression.

Confirmation along different lines can be found in the Italian cinema. In Rossellini's *Paisa* and *Germania, Anno Zero* and De Sica's *Bicycle Thieves*, Italian neo-realism stands in contrast to previous forms of cinematic realism by its elimination of any expressionism and especially by the total absence of effects obtained by editing. Just as in Welles's work (and despite their very different styles), neo-realism tends to give a film the feeling of the ambiguity of reality. The way Rossellini looks at the child's face in *Germania, Anno Zero* is at opposite poles to Kuleshov's attitude to the close-up of Moszhukhin; he wants to preserve its mystery. One should not be put on the wrong track by the fact that the evolution of neo-realism does not at first sight seem, as in America, to consist of some revolution in the technique of breaking down shots in a shooting script. There are various means of achieving the same end. Rossellini's and De Sica's are not so very spectacular, but they too aim at eliminating editing and transferring on to the screen the true continuity of reality. It is Zavattini's dream simply to film ninety consecutive minutes in the life of a man to whom nothing important happens! Luchino Visconti, the 'aesthete' of the neo-realists, revealed just as clearly as Welles the fundamental aim of his art in *La Terra Trema*, a film that is almost entirely composed of sequence-shots where the desire to take in the totality of an event can be seen in the composition in depth and the endless panning shots.

But we could not possibly examine all the films which have contributed to this linguistic evolution since 1940. It is time to draw some conclusions from what I have said. The last ten years have, I think, shown a marked progress in the field of cinematic expression. I intentionally neglected, from 1930 on, the tendency of the silent cinema that was particularly evident in Erich von Stroheim, F. W. Murnau, R. Flaherty, and Dreyer; but I do not think it died out with the coming of sound. On the contrary, I am sure it was the most fertile aspect of the so-called silent cinema, and the only one which, precisely because the essence of its aesthetic conception was not bound up with editing, called for the realism of sound as its natural extension. But it is true that the sound cinema from 1930 to 1940 owes almost nothing to it, apart from the notable and, in retrospect, prophetic exception of Jean Renoir, the only director who consistently attempted in his films up to *La Règle du Jeu* to rise above facile editing effects and seize the secret of a cinematic style which was capable of expressing everything without fragmenting the world, of revealing the hidden meaning of human beings and their environment without destroying their natural unity.

However, it would be out of the question to throw discredit on the cinema of the thirties (in any case, this would not stand up to the evidence of several masterpieces). My purpose is simply to suggest a notion of dialectical progress, the turning-point of which took place in the forties. It is true that the arrival of sound proved fatal to a certain aesthetic approach to film language, but this was an approach that was leading it farthest away from its vocation for realism. The sound cinema did however retain the essential function of editing: discontinuous description and dramatic analysis of an event. It rejected the metaphor and the symbol, and aimed instead at an illusion of objective representation. Expressionist editing almost completely disappeared, but the relative realism of that narrative style which was the general rule in 1937 contained a congenital limitation of which we could not at that time have been aware, so perfectly appropriate to it were the subjects that were treated. This was true in the case of American comedy, which reached perfection within the framework of a narrative where temporal realism played no part. Essentially logical, like vaudeville and punning, perfectly conventional in its moral and sociological content, American comedy had nothing to gain from descriptive and linear precision or from the rhythmic resources of the classical narrative style.

It is above all in the direction taken by Stroheim and Murnau, almost entirely neglected in the thirties, that the cinema has been veering more or less consciously for the last ten years. But directors are not confining themselves to prolonging it, they are deriving from it the secret of a realistic regeneration of the narrative. This narrative is again becoming capable of reintegrating the temporal truth of things, the actual duration of an event which the classical narrative insidiously replaced with intellectual and abstract time. But far from eliminating the achievements of editing once and for all, modern film-makers are giving them a relativity and a meaning. It is only when related to an increased realism in the image that extra abstraction becomes possible. The stylistic repertory of a director such as Hitchcock for example stretches from the powers of the documentary image to superimpositions and extreme close-ups. But Hitchcock's close-ups are not the same as those of Cecil B. de Mille in *The Cheat*. They are just one stylistic device among others. In other words, in the silent era, the editing *evoked* what the director wanted to say, in 1938 the narrative *described*, and today one can say that the director *writes* directly in film. The image – its plastic structure and its organisation within time – because it can now draw on greater realism, has more means at its disposal of inflecting and modifying reality from within. The film-maker is no longer simply the competitor of the painter or the playwright; he is at last the equal of the novelist.

As can be seen from this article, Bazin's approach to the cinema was a profoundly original one. He was not interested in the dry documentation of the film-historian; nor, indeed, did he ever write about a film unless he had some positive point to make (which explains the remarkable fact that he rarely panned a film – he left this to his colleagues). His approach was essentially an aesthetic one, in the original sense of the word: his starting-point was what he perceived through his senses. His next step was the analytical formulation of what he instinctively felt while watching a film. Finally, he would attempt to rationalise these feelings. His persuasiveness lies in the fact that instead of baldly stating his theory he takes the reader through all the stages of his thought and gives the impression of having just that moment discovered the truth: a truly creative method of inquiry, the archetype of which is to be found in the Essais *of Montaigne.*

It can be objected that occasionally he split ontological hairs. In his essays on eroticism and death on the screen, one feels that he perhaps allowed his reason to get the upper hand of his emotions. But the fact remains that when he was wrong about a film (which was rarely) his opinion was never the result of prejudice or preconception. He had that quality so rare in film critics: an open mind. And his likes and dislikes have almost all stood the test of time; some of them, such as his admiration of Renoir and Stroheim, were, in the mid 1940s, pioneering.

His influence on Cahiers du Cinéma *was enormous. But, as often happens, his potentially good influence did not prove in practice to be wholly so. His theories were often complex and bold; those of his disciples were more often pretentious. He was always ruthlessly clear-minded and articulate; they were often indecipherable.*

Little in Bazin recommended itself to the critics of Positif. *Extremely left-wing, they despised his 'liberal' middle-of-the-road attitude. But their main difference lay in that conflict which runs right through the history of French culture like a* basso ostinato: *the clerical versus the anti-clerical.* Positif *never forgave Bazin for being a Catholic. Perhaps they were a little too willing to blame on to him what they detested (and rightly so, I think) in his disciples. To give an idea of the sort of thing* Positif *was reacting against and why, I have included here the first extract from a very long article by Gérard Gozlan entitled, ironically of course, 'In Praise of André Bazin'.*

4: In praise of André Bazin

Gérard Gozlan

(. . .) A believer in a church, a policeman who is torturing some-body, a crying child, a woman who yields to a man, a frightened soldier – none of these, in spite of their inherent humanity, can ever stand individually as a generalised image of the human condition. Material reality envelops, pervades, and explains their basic behaviour. Reality has more than one level; it is not ambiguous, but complex and deceptive; and any attempt in art to explain or criticise it demands a search, an analysis, a choice, and an organisation. Bazin does admit the need for organisation, but only as a *pis-aller*, for in his opinion the ideal film would consist of only one shot. Since such a film is materially impossible, Bazin distinguishes certain film-makers who, although remaining faithful to editing, manage to create '*modern* works that are from an aesthetic point of view contemporaneous with the *découpage** of *Citizen Kane*, *La Règle du Jeu*, *The Little Foxes*, and *Bicycle Thieves*.' Bazin calls this new aesthetic approach *néo-montage*, and defines it as follows: 'the achievement of both physical verisimilitude and logical flexibility in the *découpage*'.

La Règle du Jeu, for instance, is an admirable attack on the bourgeoisie, but to Bazin it is 'a film that goes beyond the possibilities of editing and seizes the secret of a cinematic style that is capable of expressing everything without fragmenting the world, of

---

découpage: breakdown of a script into shots.

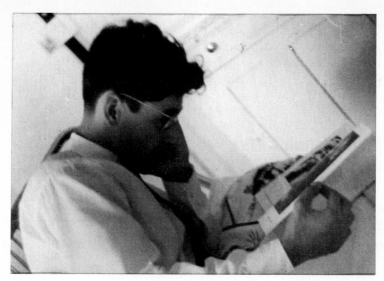

Gérard Gozlan

revealing the hidden meaning of human beings and their environment without destroying their natural unity.' And Bazin praises Hitchcock (yes, Bazin too!) because he 'excels at suggesting the ambiguity of an event while at the same time breaking it up into a series of close shots'. Ambiguity makes for a 'liberal and democratic' style *par excellence*: 'the director who breaks down the scenario into shots for us makes the choice that we ourselves make in real life. We unconsciously accept his analysis because it conforms with the way we look at a film; but on the other hand it does deprive us of a privilege that has just as strong a psychological basis – and which we give up without realising we are doing so – i.e. the freedom, or virtual freedom anyway, to modify our own system of breaking down reality at any given moment.' Should one conclude from this mumbo-jumbo that Bazin feels that when there *is* analysis the spectator is being cheated, and the meaning he gets from the film comes to him only via his subconscious? But when no analysis is done for the spectator, lo and behold! he actively tries to analyse, and actually gets close to the truth, as he is 'free to do his own *mise-en-scène*.' The interest and attentiveness of the spectator is multiplied ten times: this, one supposes, is psychological freedom. He is given back his independence: this is another kind of freedom, moral freedom. In other words, suppose there are thirty people listening to a lecture; it is quite natural that those who best understand what the lecturer is talking about will be those who are interested in what he is saying. But it does not go without saying that they understand better because the lecturer is talking about his subject 'objectively', or without any previously thought out ideas, or without any kind of developed analysis. One may even go so far as to question the validity of a word such as 'objectivity' in connection with religion. And what if one of the thirty listeners, left free to do his own *mise-en-scène*, wants to look at the flies buzzing round the room or at the colour of the walls? Can one then say that he is nearer the truth than his neighbour, who possesses a certain knowledge of what the lecturer is talking about and will have certain 'opinions' about it?

I suppose the answer would be that this is a more moral way of going about things, it is 'democracy'. In analytical editing, writes Bazin, 'the spectator simply follows his guide, and lets his attention identify itself with that of the director, who choses for him what he should see'; whereas when one enters the realm of the *découpage* passivity is replaced by that 'minimum of personal choice' on the part of the spectator. That is why Bazin praises Wyler in *The Best Years of Our Lives*, because 'an ethical scrupulousness for reality is given an aesthetic transcription in the *mise-en-scène*', and he adds that 'the only way to imitate Wyler would be to espouse the ethics of *mise-en-scène* that have produced their finest results in *The Best Years of Our Lives*'.

I propose to examine a specific example of a shot which is remarkable for the way in which depth of field is used and the *mise-en-scène* organised within a single frame. It occurs in Robert Aldrich's *The Garment Jungle*. The scene takes place in the trade union's headquarters; Renata, the extremist leader, is haranguing his comrades. Suddenly a group of blacklegs in the pay of the

The union meeting in *The Garment Jungle*

employers burst in and break up the meeting. Then comes the following shot: on the far left, in extreme close-up and facing the camera, is the leader of the blacklegs, Renata is in the centre of the frame, and in the background are the union members seated on benches with the blacklegs watching them. This is just the sort of *mise-en-scène* that Bazin likes; for here the spectator is not forced by the editing to watch what the director has chosen for him – he is free to look at what he wishes: the killer, or Renata, who refuses to give in, or the people in the background, who are immobile or threatening. But we must remember that whatever freedom is given the spectator to do his own little *mise-en-scène*, nothing will be changed in Aldrich's *mise-en-scène*, which is the only one that counts. And Aldrich's *mise-en-scène* in this shot is absolutely inseparable from the context, i.e. what is important for him is the aggressive confrontation of two men, with the mass of union members wavering between them. The spectator's job is not simply to watch what he wants to, and say afterwards that he has the right to cuddle up to his girl-friend, but to perceive the conflict that Aldrich has so remarkably grouped within a single frame: the struggle between a man who represents the workers and a man who has sold himself to the employers.

Does the depth of composition and the organisation of most of the characters within the same frame prove that reality is ambiguous and all on the same level? Not a bit of it. For Aldrich could equally well have given us a succession of shots of the killer, and then of Renata, with reaction shots of the union members – the content would have remained the same, i.e. the ferocious opposition of two men and two classes. Why did Aldrich shoot it as he did? Certainly not in order to give the scene a stylishly modern look, and certainly not because he had been reading Bazin, but simply because the opposition is more striking when shown in this way. The presence in the foreground of the killer's face, which Renata cannot see, makes the latter's position even more fragile and precarious, and suggests the power of the repressive machine. And so depth of composition here does not introduce a new way of conceiving or apprehending reality (editing would have been able to do the same thing too), but simply allows the film-maker to draw on a greater range of stylistic means to describe reality as he feels it. Some of Bazin's disciples would like to suppress cross-cutting entirely, as though it were necessary to attack the very nature of cross-cutting, instead of its unintelligent use. For if, in several of Carné's films, cross-cutting rapidly becomes a tiring device, it is probably because the framing each time gives us no more than a simple shot of each character, so that the *découpage*, instead of enriching the relationship that has already been created between the two characters by dialogue, gestures, and the sets, deprives us of some of this interplay. There is no question of metaphysics or fundamental principles here.

And yet it is the transition to metaphysics that is important for Bazin. Proof of this is to be found in the way he explains the poisoning scene in *Citizen Kane*. According to Bazin, thanks to the depth of composition, the spectator's eye can roam freely between the glass in the foreground and the door at the other end of the

'The spectator's eye can roam freely between the glass in the foreground and the door at the other end of the room, which is opened by Kane'

room, which is opened by Kane. The continuity of the spectator's gaze leads, I suppose, straight to the assertion that 'all reality is on the same level'. This again is patently specious thinking, for Bazin leaps from a dramatic meaning that is a specific part of the scene and of the film as a whole to a very general meaning, the most general possible – and also highly debatable. The result is a levelling down of the elements of reality, instead of a demonstration of their organisation, their opposition, and their true relationship. It is no mere coincidence that Bazin's and Wyler's paths crossed: Wyler's style has the same tendency to level down, to iron out differences, while putting the *mise-en-scène* on a level where relationships, conflicts, and contradictions are highly superficial. Nor is it a mere coincidence that Bazin defines Wyler's *mise-en-scène* as an 'attempt to suppress itself', and talks of a 'negative definition' of *mise-en-scène*.

But let's get back to the role of the spectator. Bazin demands that he be given 'freedom', i.e. a kind of virginity regained, a completely new purity in the face of the mystery of screen reality. The free man should be something like a mind that has been completely emptied of the farrago it has acquired and learned; it must be ready to re-learn everything from scratch, in that ideal and sacred place, the cinema. The film spectator is a new being, and one should be able to conceive of him as being something outside the other elements of reality. Let's take Kuleshov's experiment. It will be agreed that Moszhukhin's face is remarkable for one thing only: it is inexpressive, in so far as expression necessarily implies some sort of content. Why then does Bazin substitute the word 'ambiguous' for the word 'inexpressive'? 'Kuleshov's experiment', writes Bazin, 'gives a precise meaning each time to the face whose ambiguity has made possible these alternately exclusive interpretations.' The fallacy lies in that arbitrary and purely verbal substitution which, for Bazin, but only for Bazin, implies a dubious metaphysical idea, that of ambiguity. The fallacy also lies in a highly debatable belief in the 'passive' role of the spectator. Bazin's whole reasoning presupposes that the nature of editing, by tampering with reality, renders the spectator's behaviour completely passive. For it should be said that an actor's expression is suggested to the spectator not so much by the nature of editing as by the spectator's own psychological make-up. I should be very surprised, for example, if a seven-year-old child or a homosexual were to attribute the same passion to Moszhukhin when he 'looks' at the naked woman as would a non-homosexual adult. And since the range of characteristics in any audience is very wide, it is probable that each spectator, according to the interest he has in the woman on the screen, will see on Moszhukhin's face a greater or lesser expression of desire. One can see that the famous 'shadow' projected by the nature of editing on the 'spectator's consciousness' is pure invention, since even in this example of schematic editing – Kuleshov's laboratory experiment – the spectator's behaviour must be much richer than Bazin suggests. No one, if one can put it this way, is virgin soil.

Perhaps Bazin was simply naïve. Some of those who knew him believe this to be so. It is not difficult to agree with them, on the evidence of this quotation from his book, *De Sica*, published in

Italy: 'In order to paint every blade of grass one has to be a Douanier Rousseau.' But when a naïve person 'attempts to find in the cinema a substitute for his religious faith' (as Claude Brémond puts it in an excellent article in the sociological review *Communications* [No. 1, pp. 211 ff.]), and analyses it so lamentably while remaining skilful enough to avoid talking about realities, how can we distinguish between *naïveté* and mystification? 'Bazin reminds one of the pious believer,' Brémond goes on 'who comes back from a pilgrimage to the Holy Places without suspecting the trafficking that goes on in the Court of the Temple. One admires his Faith, but not his talents as a sociological observer.'

When Bazin invokes 'the metaphysical assertion that all reality exists on the same level,' there is no point in trying seriously to find out what he means by that, or where he unearthed this 'assertion'. Put simply, and less indulgently, it could be said that Bazin's whole system does not begrudge us metaphysical assertions. However many flow glibly from his tongue, there are always others to take their place. One only needs to read a few lines of Bazin to recognise that while some of the ideas are of uncertain origin, others have been all too obviously assimilated from Lachelier, Lavelle, Saint Augustine, and Teilhard de Chardin. Everything is chucked haphazardly into the melting-pot, in the hope that the essence of that marvellous medium, the cinema, will emerge. We get, as a result, mere jargon rather than vocabulary, linguistic tics and clap-trap rather than solid thought. In almost any connection, he will use religious vocabulary in a foolhardy but revealing manner. Bazin considers the Cannes Film Festival to be 'an order', and talks of 'Holy Places, priesthood, vespers, and matins'. A bullfight is 'the mystic triangle of animal, man, and multitude', accompanied by a 'liturgy and an almost religious feeling'. In Nicolai Ekk's *The Way to Life*, rehabilitation is treated as 'purification through trust and love, a conversion which has the instantaneity of divine grace'. For Lamprecht's *Emil and the Detectives*, Bazin evokes the 'famous chase of the bad man through the streets, which takes on the epic grandeur of a celestial cohort harrying Evil'. The world is characterised by its 'folly'. He talks only of 'cleansing, purifying, washing,

Emil and the Detectives

and excising' such things as 'obscenity, defilement, filth, and decay', and the cinema is entrusted with the not very savoury task of being 'a vernicle on the face of human suffering'. Like faith, 'the irrational power of photography carries conviction', realism is a 'regeneration' of the narrative, 'asceticism' triumphs, and 'revelation' too; the director tries to pierce the 'fabric' of the exterior world, and 'administers love and friendship to his creatures'.

There can be no question of leaving André Bazin without making a little pilgrimage to the monthly magazine of which he was one of the pillars. The disciples of Bazin, no less than their master, have emitted, and are still emitting, gigantic blasts of hot air. And so in this part of my article, Moullet, Mourlet, Godard, Douchet, and many others will be our guests. People will certainly object to the fact that I have not always quoted the directors or the films to which the disciples refer, and will claim that this 'distorts' my inquiry. I have consciously avoided such references in most cases, for when the disciples talk about films and directors, they are such experts at talking about something completely different that what I have done

A Bout de Souffle

is rather a service to the films and their directors.

The members of the Holy Family (that unparalleled magazine *Cahiers du Cinéma*, hereafter abbreviated to CC) believe in the 'metaphysical evil' (Eric Rohmer, CC 61, p. 8) of human creatures which 'agitates a world where night reigns unchallenged' (Jean Douchet, CC 81, p. 53). By virtue of this 'immediate, eternal and terrifying, conflict between Light and Darkness' (Douchet, CC 99, p. 46), colour is experienced as an inconvenience or at least as a superfluous element, in a context where black and white directly reveals the essential and does not need to take the iridescent but roundabout way of concrete realism' (Michel Mourlet, CC 99, p. 22); 'the implacable struggle of white against black, the masses of shadows that criss-cross and collide, streaked with white flashes' (Charles Bitsch CC 51, p. 43) swamp Douchet himself, who, having declared that night reigns unchallenged, now states that 'darkness has invaded light', and elsewhere that 'light has totally absorbed darkness, and remains perceptible only as a false glow, a deceptive semblance – woolly, glazed, and glaucous' (CC 81, p. 53). Rivette, who also has trouble in seeing clearly, incriminates 'the grimace of the world' (CC, 25, p. 45).

From this first episode, which must have been written during a power strike, you will probably have realised that their point is to make sinners feel that 'man bears the stigmata of his malediction' and that 'he wanders in a world bereft for ever of true light' (Douchet, CC 81, p. 53). We are all guilty, and pretty big sinners, it is true. The Catholic Alfred Hitchcock likes to illustrate this postulate. However, things always turn out for the better, since *I Confess* 'tells the story of a soul that is invincibly attached to the Light by willpower' (Douchet, CC 99, p. 46). 'In this struggle, one which materialism might be expected to have won in advance, it is the soul that emerges the victor' (Rohmer, CC 69, p. 44). Rohmer talks of that 'quality of anguish which *Ordet* makes us experience' (CC 55, p. 28), of that 'special air we breathe' in Nicholas Ray's *Bigger Than Life*, of 'the faith we can read in the eyes' of the characters, 'faith that is riddled with doubts and yet is ever-present' (CC 69, p. 44). Henri Agel demands of us 'a *different* kind of attentiveness' (CC 53, p. 50), and Michel Mardore speaks of 'that poetry of another order which introduces rigour into the secret disposition of a vision of the world that is more esoteric at a secondary level than its superficial commotions allow us to glimpse' (CC 125, p. 51). Then the Holy Family intones the Midnight Mass: 'It is not so much a *Miserere* as a *De Profundis* in the strict sense of the term (from the depths of the abyss I have called to you, O Lord!) that we feel rising during the first part of *Il Bidone*, until it spreads and spurts in our eyes like pus from an abscess' (Agel, CC 58, p. 34).

In the ideal cinema and in masterpieces, 'the truth is their truth' (Jean-Luc Godard, CC 85, p. 1). 'Everything here seems to grow from its own base through a perfect spontaneity towards itself and yet in perfect conformity with things exterior' (Beylie, CC 84, p. 52). And since everything, in this cinema of 'oblation' (Agel, CC 67, p. 45) is for the best in the best of all possible worlds, we need only to follow 'that irrepressible rising curve towards a certain level of ecstasy' (Rivette, CC 81, p. 30), or, if you prefer, 'integrate the meanderings of emotion in an infinitely extensible decorative fabric, or better even, freely extract from the plastic totality of the audio-visual field the conducting narrative motif, only to let it plunge back and hear it resound, or finally – and here we are coming back to a refined kind of neo-realism – extract from the general human atmosphere the obsessional elements that certainly lurk there' (Beylie, CC 91, p. 62). Agel goes into raptures about Renoir's *The River*, 'the moving modulation of a voice that says yes, of a soul that consents to the world, that has passed the stage of revolt', and François Truffaut praises these lines, 'the most pertinent that have been written about *The River*' (CC 45, p. 56). The story that counts is the one 'told by Murnau and Rossellini, about man reaching a state of acquiescence, and through it, oneness' (Demonsablon, CC 95, p. 2). And Mizoguchi, according to Rivette, is representative of an 'art of modulation, whereby everything finally harmonises with this search for a central point where appearances and what is called nature (or shame or death) are reconciled with man' (CC 81, p. 30). Technique is put to the service of this spiritual Oneness: Agel talks of 'the spiritual engagement' that is sustained by tracking shots (admiringly quoted by Truffaut (CC 45, p. 56)), and Rivette, when discussing Astruc, compares 'the movements of the camera to the movements of the soul' and arrives at a 'veritable mystique of the tracking crane shot' (CC 52, p. 47).

These totally fatuous remarks are strongly reminiscent of the speeches of the princes that govern us. For only someone who assumes that colonial wars are the unhealthy external appearance of French good health will say that 'Ray's films end where Rossellini's begin: with the intuition of a harmony that is to be found beyond the sphere of conflicts and clashes of opinion' (Demonsablon, CC 95, p. 55). Rivette speaks of 'a bargain that is never broken' (CC 81, p. 30), and Beylie, using language that could easily be pornographic, sings the praises of Renoir's 'exertion, which might be termed encyclopaedic if it did not go hand in hand with a rejection of academicism in a resolutely constructive sense, and which jettisons subsidiary arborescences only to rise more easily, straight up, and full of sap, into the serene sky of aesthetic transcendency' (CC 80, p. 1).

The end of *Pickpocket*

There is no point in our readers wasting their time wondering about the truth of these assertions, since we are now in the domain of pure beauty, pure spirit, and aesthetic transcendency, where 'the true is as false as the false, and only the ultra-false becomes true' (Moullet, CC 87, p. 56). Opinions and attitudes shed all materiality: 'To watch Renoir's characters living is to adopt a better point of view about man, to live better and to be more oneself, to attain, slowly but surely, a kind of serenity' (Beylie, CC 80, p. 8). Materiality becomes a 'shimmer', 'an immense and multiple symphony' (Beylie, CC 80, p. 8), 'a reflection of the divine, a perfect possession of the world and of oneself, a moment like pure water taking the shape of the contours of a vase' (Mourlet, CC 98, p. 34). 'The soul is the key to the universe' (Douchet, CC 99, p. 45). Life and the world are conceived henceforth as an 'exchange', 'correspondence', 'secret effluvia that emanate from beings' (Rivette, CC 52, p. 47). Perhaps that is why when one gets to the last shot of *Pickpocket*, 'although

Ingrid Bergman in *Europe 51*

the bars separate the two heroes (the man and the woman), their *souls* have found one another' (Jean Wagner, CC 104, p. 50). You can lose everything, but you still have heaven.

A woman, just as she was on the first day when God created her, is a woman, i.e. permanently guilty, as the existence of adultery goes to prove. Dorsday allows us to psycho-analyse the Holy Family when he states: 'In Buñuel's *El*, the man's jealousy is only an exalted form of his purity' (CC 37, p. 44), a 'purity' which the woman cannot understand, as she is 'by nature incapable of attaining sublimity or responsibility', 'the whole business could have been avoided but for her', and although she may have 'the face of love, she does not have the soul of love'; the woman is the 'symbol of the evil of the world' (CC 37, p. 44). If a woman takes a lover who is sound in body and soul, she is well and truly sinful in the eyes of the Holy Family, whereas a saintly woman who rejects the temptations of the flesh is innocent: 'In *Europe 51*, the soul (of Ingrid

Bergman) fully reveals itself, bathes her body in light, forms it in its own image, and surrounds it with an aura of brightness that makes everything which comes near look dull and pale' (Rohmer, CC 25, p. 44). Even more innocent is a woman who is decomposing, a woman on her deathbed: 'if she knows how to die, nothing is lost'; on her deathbed, indeed, woman is no longer made up of 'spasms' and 'pleasure', she becomes 'an interior irradiation', and that is sufficient to save an age that is 'trying to redeem itself' (collective introduction to the special CC issue on 'Woman and the Cinema'). Just as the best Indian is a dead Indian, the best woman is a dead woman.

The governing idea is that great films 'are able to offer and conceal the secret of a world of which they are at once the sole trustee and fascinating reflection' (Godard, CC 85, p. 1), and they all 'end with the serene joy of someone who has overcome the illusory phenomena of perspectives' (Rivette, CC 81, p. 30). Do not be surprised that 'loving Renoir is rather the same thing as loving the movements of the stars, the song of the birds, or the beating of a heart in the breast of a woman' (Beylie, CC 80, p. 8), and you will find all that enclosed in the heart of a film like *Le Carrosse d'Or*, which contains the Truth like 'a starfish that opens and closes' (Godard, CC 85, p. 1). Nothing exists except the cinema, which is the currency of the Absolute: 'There used to be theatre (Griffith), poetry (Murnau), painting (Rossellini), dance (Eisenstein), music (Renoir). But from now on there is cinema. And the cinema is Nicholas Ray' (Godard, CC 79, p. 44). One can even go so far as to say, with Godard, that '*Bitter Victory*, just as the sun makes you close your eyes, is not cinema, it is more than cinema', 'blind truth' (Godard, CC 79, p. 45). This approach to films has set off a fashion, and Michel Delahaye begins an article by blinding the reader: 'How can one approach *Elmer Gantry*, a work at once classical and meteoric? The best way is probably the simplest: let's make it quite clear from the start that we are dealing with a work that quite literally *dazzles*' (CC 121, p. 51). The atheist and the rationalist are, of course, free *not* to believe, 'everyone has the right to give a non-Catholic view of a Catholic film' (Demonsablon, CC 58, p. 40), but then he must not be surprised to find merely 'the spectacle of a godless world in which the only law is the pure mechanism of cause and effect, a universe of cruelty, horror, banality, and derision' (Rohmer, CC 25, p. 45).

But follow their advice and 'yield to the facts instead of wanting to shape them' (Rivette, CC 58, p. 41), 'let yourself be taken over by the order of things' (Mourlet, CC 111, p. 34), do not protest, and 'you will be liberated from everyday cares', sheltered and far from a world which 'if it has not been irremediably condemned, at least seems, in the eyes of Hitchcock, to be increasingly suspect' (Rivette, CC 58, p. 41). 'All is dust and will return to dust' (Godard, CC 97, p. 44), the Last Judgement is imminent, and in *The Trouble With Harry* 'the russet leaves of autumn somehow presage the decay of nature, and almost stand for that decay itself' (Rivette, CC 58, p. 41). And so what does it matter where 'one chooses to escape from the mesh of circumstances – a prison, an asylum, the maquis, a monastery?' (Beylie, CC 122, p. 54). 'Directing a film and writing a scenario consists of pointing the eye of the camera on faces and objects long enough to brand them deeply, as the torturer used to brand his prisoner, or as a sign from Him marks the chosen one' (Godard, CC 95, p. 56). In this kind of conception of existence, where everything is put in parentheses so that God can be reached more rapidly, 'it is no longer a question of reality or fiction, but of something completely different, the stars in the sky perhaps, and men who like to gaze at the stars and dream. What are such things as love, fear, contempt, danger, adventure, despair, bitterness, victory? What importance do they have in comparison with the stars?' (Godard, CC 79, p. 45).

Faced with such self-confidence, we begin to doubt the non-existence of God. What on earth has happened to Bazin's famous theories about 'ambiguity'. Ambiguity is certainly not what we will find in Cecil B. De Mille, one of the all-time greats according to Godard, and praised because 'the moral of *The Ten Commandments* is extraordinarily manicheistic – just a straight line, no dialectics: Rameses stands for Mao Tse-tung, and Moses for De Mille himself' (CC 80, p. 58). Perhaps we will find it in Samuel Fuller then, 'a

master of ambiguity' (Domarchi, CC 57, p. 50). This means, according to Godard, that although Fuller is 'apparently a nationalist, a reactionary, a Nixonite', he is too endowed 'with the gift of ambiguity to belong exclusively to any one party' (Moullet, CC 93, p. 13). 'He is more concerned with fascism as a trait of character than with its political consequences' (Moullet, CC 93, p. 13), which completely fails to explain a film such as *Hell and High Water*, but don't let's press our point. . . . It is well known that politics do not interest the Holy Family any more than they do Fuller, and Hawks is praised by Godard because *Rio Bravo* simply expresses 'the finest of morals: that a man should earn his daily bread and not care about the rest' (CC 97, p. 44). The only thing that matters is 'the moral of duty in the work one does, whereby one rejects laziness, inexactitude, and perfunctoriness' (Domarchi, CC 79, p. 51), in a world 'where a person can happen to be a sheriff just as well as a skilled worker or a ticket-collector' (Moullet, CC 97, p. 44). 'Rossellini's realism is moral realism' (Domarchi, CC 123, p. 60). Why tamper with the 'vulnerability' (Agel, CC 67, p. 45) of these 'simple faces, these gusts of humanity, these furtive expressions, these snatches of life seized almost at random from human beings, this confidence, this "you'll-see-if-it-doesn't-turn-out-all-right" attitude' (Patrice G. Hovald *Italian Neo-Realism*, Editions du Cerf). The Brasillach* branch of the Holy Family celebrates Mass in rather a different way: 'If art is basically moral [*sic*], it does not become so by showing the way to abstract equality or freedom, but rather by exalting the exception that is made possible only by the rule, and as it were, however shocking this idea may be, the inequality of every man in the face of his destiny, or rather of his salvation' (Rohmer, CC 26, p. 18). 'Lang is fascinated only by the exceptional being, who though exceptional is modestly given the humble appearance of a dancing-girl, a female spy, a cop, or a tough cowboy' (Truffaut, CC 31, p. 52). 'The political ideas of Brasillach were the same as Drieu La Rochelle's; ideas which result in their authors being sentenced to death are necessarily estimable' (Truffaut, CC 32, p. 59).

*Robert Brasillach, a right-wing film critic and historian, was shot after the Liberation for having collaborated with the Germans (Ed.).

The Trouble with Harry

I could go on for much longer; *Cahiers du Cinéma* is an inexhaustible fund of phraseology and gags. But it will not make our grandchildren laugh; no one laughs nowadays at the complete works of Henri Bataille – they are simply not read any more. Well, it is worth pointing out that the man Rohmer sees as the spiritual father of *Cahiers* is none other than Bazin: 'Everything had been said by him, we came too late. Now we are left with the difficult duty of pursuing his task: we shall not fail in this, although we are convinced that he pursued it much further than it will be possible for us to do ourselves. . . . Only the uncertainty of the future authorises us to hope that we are, if not André Bazin's successors, then at least his disciples, and not too unworthy ones at that' (Rohmer, CC 91, p. 45). In this part of my argument, I will say no more. As barristers say, my case rests.

It may of course be argued that one can prove almost anything when one quotes out of context. But I think Gozlan's procedure is legitimate. Where I have checked the reviews he quotes from, none of them has been deformed. This is because Gozlan's aim is less to prove a case, to move from point to logical point, than to evoke the atmosphere and tone of Cahiers *during a certain period.*

However, it would be only fair, I think, to quote here a couple of the texts in their entirety. The first, Claude Chabrol's notorious plea for the 'little theme', contains a lot of hard common sense. But it is marred by Chabrol's jemenfoutiste *('couldn't-care-less') attitude and conscious prejudice against the ambitious theme* per se. *A similar, and equally persuasive, article could be written, containing just as great a proportion of truth and falsehood, championing the big, as against the little, theme. The second article, Jean-Luc Godard's review of Astruc's* Une Vie, *is remarkable for a number of reasons. Not only is its tone, blustering, halting, pretentious, and full of paradoxes, very close to that of the films he was later to make; but Godard, who sees the universe in his own very personal terms, spots in Astruc's film (or more likely reads into it) some of the characteristics of his own work: abrupt changes of tone, gratuitousness, gestures and acts seen out of context, almost abstractly.*

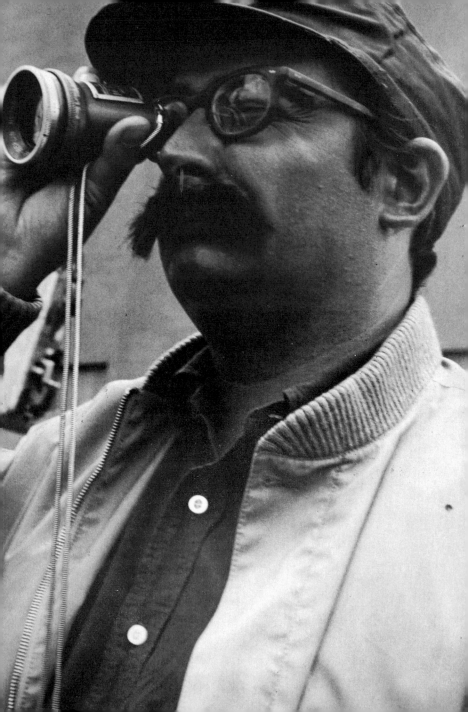

5: Little themes

Claude Chabrol

Anyone who wants to make a film on a theme of his own choosing has two solutions open to him. Depending on his aspirations the film-maker can describe the French Revolution or a quarrel with the next-door neighbours, the apocalypse of our time or the barmaid who gets herself pregnant, the final hours of a hero of the Resistance or an inquiry into the murder of a prostitute. It is a question of personality: the important thing, surely, is that the film should be good, that it should be well directed and well constructed, that it should be good cinema. The only distinction one can make between the apocalypse and the prostitute, the revolution and the barmaid, the hero and the quarrelling neighbours is on the level of the ambitiousness of the theme. For there *are*, of course, big and little themes. Anyone who doesn't agree should put up his hand.

From here on, it's child's play: it is easy to tell which film deserves one's attention and which one does not. I take two sheets of paper, and on one I write the following synopsis:

The Apocalypse of Our Time. Scenario: After a total atomic war, life has disappeared from the face of the earth. The sole survivor is a Negro, all alone in New York. He organises his life as best he can, but suffers from loneliness. After a couple of months he realises that another human being, a white woman, has survived the catastrophe. He meets her. Soon he falls in love with her, but his racial complexes make happiness impossible for him. Two months later,

73

a white man appears in a dinghy. He too wants the woman. At first the Negro acts self-effacingly, then he reacts and challenges the other man. The white man decides on a duel to the death, and in the deserted city, in front of the United Nations building, the two last men on earth throw themselves into the final struggle. For it is, of course, war, man's folly, that is 'the apocalypse of our time'.

On the other sheet of paper I write this:

The Quarrel Between Neighbours. Scenario: In an isolated part of the Causses, a poor farmer lives alone. He has organised his life as best he can, but he suffers from loneliness. One day, another human being, a woman from the city, appears. Her car has broken down. She yields to the charms of the countryside. The farmer does her the honours of the house and shows her his primitive life on the land. Soon he falls in love with her, but his peasant status, compared with her status as a city-dweller, makes happiness impossible for him. A little later, a former farmer, who has lived in the city for some time, decides to return to the land. He settles down on the neighbouring farm, and soon he too wants the woman. To start with, the first farmer acts self-effacingly; then he reacts and challenges the other man, who thereupon decides on a duel to the death. In the desolate windswept Causses, in the shadow of the wild Cevennes mountains, the two men fight. For it is, of course, true that farmers enjoy a 'good quarrel with their neighbour'.

I compare the two sheets of paper, get my friends to read them, submit them to producers. There's no doubt about it: *The Apocalypse of Our Time* is a big theme, and *The Quarrel Between Neighbours* is a banal and worthless story. I shoot *The Apocalypse*, and the result is the biggest load of tripe for years. Everyone is amazed, and no one more than I. However, some people are gullible enough to be taken in: maybe the film is imperfect, but the subject is of such importance that everyone should be interested in it. They proclaim: '*The Apocalypse of Our Time* is interesting for several reasons.' But although I may be a sucker, I can recognise a good film when I see one, and I realise that my life's work is indeed of little worth.

In a flash of clear-sightedness, I have another look at *The Quarrel Between Neighbours* and I realise the subject is the same; I also realise that it doesn't hold water. Once shorn of its apocalyptic setting and brought down to earth, *The Apocalypse of Our Time* doesn't belong to our time or to any other. As *The Quarrel Between Neighbours* proves, it does not point to a social, psychological, or even metaphysical truth of any kind. *The Apocalypse* was rubbish, as was *The Quarrel Between Neighbours*, and for the same reasons.

This is what I am getting at: quite apart from any cinematic considerations, which are irrelevant here, a big theme is no more valuable than a small one. It is a decoy which from time to time becomes a booby-trap.

To take my argument a little further, it wasn't at all the theme that was big in the story of the Apocalypse, for the same sequence of events can result in the most inept of peasant dramas. The setting is a camouflage: a deserted city does not offer any greater cinematic possibilities than the Causses – on the contrary – but the cretin who has seen neither of them is impressed.

Look, cretin, here are the traps into which you fall: the big themes.

An *exhaustive* list of big themes:

(a) Big Historical Themes:

Adam and Eve (especially if they are not shown naked). Certain allegories are allowed on condition the names of the characters are explicit: Eve or Eva, with Adam as a surname. The serpent is of course the seducer.

Joan of Arc, and by extension: saintliness, the big-hearted or heroic prostitute (Nurse Marthe Richard is on duty, a Resistance fighter, she sleeps with Hitler to steal some documents from him, a victim of the cold war), children, mothers, and a general.

The French Revolution, and the one which is still continuing throughout the world, the class struggle, strikes, suffragettes, equal rights for women.

Wars, which everyone hates, but which do produce heroes, good causes, and bad ones too. Joan of Arc can easily be included under this heading.

The atomic bomb, the apocalypse of our time.

(b) Big Human Themes:

Love, characterised by the problem of the couple (without the intervention of the serpent): brief encounters, subtle changes of heart.

The Brotherhood of Man: I am my brother's keeper, and I take heed lest he fall.

Mine Own Executioner: sunk to the bottom of the abyss, and now a man, he finds the strength to climb up again.

The Green Paradise: the mysteries of childhood and life, the conflict between innocence and the adult world.

Death: he looks back over his life and dies of shame. He was too cold, he didn't love his fellow men.

God: I leave the Church, thou leavest the Church, he leaves the Church. Why are we all leaving the Church?

That's all.

In my opinion, there's no such thing as a big theme and a little theme, because the smaller the theme is, the more one can give it a big treatment. The truth is, truth is all that matters.

Stanley Kramer's *The Defiant Ones:* Big Human Theme

6: Review of Astruc's *Une Vie*

Jean-Luc Godard

I couldn't care less about the merry-go-round, with its Walt Disney-type decoration, the lunch on the grass with its plastic imitation table-cloths, the ball of wool that is the colour of chewing-gum. I couldn't care less about all the lapses in taste that Astruc, Claude Renoir, and Mayo have committed. And as for Roman Vlad's saxophone. . . . Actually, he plays rather well. But in any case the beauty of *Une Vie* lies elsewhere.

It lies in the yellow dress of Pascale Petit as she shivers amidst the Velazquez-grey dunes of Normandy. 'That's not true, they aren't Velazquez-grey! Nor Delacroix-grey for that matter,' the 'connoisseurs' will squawk.

But in vain. Already Christian Marquand is leaning over the end of the jetty and holding out his hand to Maria Schell. The 'connoisseurs' are foxed by a film that moves so quickly it seems almost to be running on the spot. It is well known that the fastest racing cars are those that have the best brakes: so it is with *Une Vie*. One thought one knew Astruc; one started building up theories, without noticing that the sequence was over and that the film had gone off in another aesthetic or moral direction. One talked of Velazquez without noticing that Pascale Petit's dress was Baudelaire-yellow and Maria Schell's eyes Ramuz-blue. Why Ramuz? Because behind Maupassant's cardboard characters, behind Jeanne and Julien, it is the face of 'Aline' or of 'Jean-Luc Persécuté' that Astruc is filming. There is nothing surprising in this, for it is well known that Astruc

79

has long admired the author of *Signes Parmi Nous*. And why did I also mention the author of *The Albatross* just now? Because the first shot of *Une Vie* gives the whole film a Baudelairean stamp. Because Maria Schell runs down to the sea as fast as her legs will carry her and Pascale Petit's dress echoes the most famous line of the poet who said to Manet: 'You are the foremost in the decadence of your art.' One could also mention Thomas Hardy, Faulkner too, and the Charlotte Rittenmayer of *Wild Palms*, who can be seen here transposed in the character played by Marquand; but Astruc himself said so much about this (perhaps too much) that the admirers of *Le Rideau Cramoisi* have started frantically searching for something which they have been surprised not to find. What does all this prove? Simply that I was talking about painting without realising that *Une Vie* is the film of a novelist, and about taste without realising that it is the film of an uncouth director.

Well there we are, I have defended the film against those who admire it for the wrong reasons. As for the others, my task is easier; *Une Vie* is almost the opposite of the typical Astruc film, in so far as we had confined Astruc to a prefabricated aesthetic system which he has now broken out of.

Who cares if the version now being shown in cinemas bears little or no resemblance to the one intended by the scenario? Who cares if each scene is systematically cut short just at its climax by the editing? *Une Vie* must be admired as it stands. And, as it stands, *Une Vie* doesn't look very much like an inspired film. Madness behind realism, Astruc has said in an interview. But he has been misunderstood. Julien was mad to have married Jeanne, and Jeanne mad to have married Julien. And that's that. The idea was not to show *La Folie du Docteur Tube*, but to show how silly it was for a man of the open air to fall in love with a domesticated woman. As a matter of fact, *Une Vie* worries Astruc's most enthusiastic admirers, just as *Le Plaisir* worried those who thought they knew their Maupassant. People expected Astruc to be lyrical, whereas what they got was Astruc the architect.

Une Vie is a superbly constructed film. So may I, in order to illustrate my point, use terms borrowed from classical geometry.

A film may be compared to a *geometrical locus*, i.e. a group of points that possess the same property in relation to a fixed element. This group of points is, if you like, the *mise-en-scène*; and that single property common to every moment of the *mise-en-scène* is the scenario, or, if you prefer, the dramatic outline. All that's left is the fixed element (which may possibly even be mobile): the subject. Well, what happens is this: with most film-makers, the geometrical locus of the subjects they claim to treat never extends beyond the place of shooting. What I mean is that the action of their film may very well take place over an enormous area, but most film-makers never *conceive* their *mise-en-scène* in terms which extend beyond the limits of the set. Astruc, on the other hand, gives one the feeling he has conceived his film over the whole area demanded by the scenario, no more no less. We see only three or four Normandy landscapes in *Une Vie*. And yet the film gives one the uncanny feeling it has been *thought out on the true scale of Normandy*, just as *Tabu* was on the scale of the Pacific and *Que Viva Mexico!* on that of Mexico. Perhaps I am over-interpreting the evidence; but the evidence is there. The fact is too remarkable to leave unmentioned. And all the more so as Astruc and Laudenbach did not make things easier for themselves by showing, as I said, only three or four aspects of the woods of Normandy. For the difficulty was not to show the forest, but to show a drawing-room which one *knew* was only a few yards away from the forest. What was even more difficult was not to show the sea, but to show a bedroom which one *knew* was only half a mile from the sea. Most films are constructed on the few square yards of décor that are visible through the viewfinder. *Une Vie* has been conceived, written, and directed over five acres.

Astruc has set up his dramatic and visual coordinates over this vast invisible area. Between the abscissa and the ordinate there is no curve that might reveal some secret progression in the film. The only curve is either the abscissa or the ordinate – which in fact adds up to two kinds of progression, one horizontal, the other vertical. The whole *mise-en-scène* of *Une Vie* has this basic principle as its axis. Maria Schell and Pascale Petit's dash down to the shore is horizontal. Marquand bending down to help his partner on to the

jetty of the port is vertical. The exit of the married couple after the wedding feast is horizontal. The stroke of the knife that rips open the bodice is vertical. Again, the movement of Jeanne and Julien rolling in the corn is horizontal; that of Marquand's hand seizing Antonella Lualdi's wrist is vertical. And so on. For Astruc, the *mise-en-scène* of *Une Vie* lay quite simply in emphasising one of these two movements, horizontal or vertical, in every scene or shot that had its own dramatic unity, and in doing so in an *abrupt* way, so that all that did not form part of this abrupt movement sank into the background before or after it.

In *Les Mauvaises Rencontres*, Astruc was still using this kind of effect, this carefully thought out recourse to violence, in the manner of Bardem: on a cut, on a door that opens, a glass that breaks, a face that turns away. In *Une Vie*, on the other hand, he uses it in mid-shot, extending the technique of Brooks and particularly Nicholas Ray so far that *the effect becomes almost the cause*. What is beautiful is not so much Marquand dragging Maria Schell out of the château as the suddenness of the gestures that give the suspense of the film a new lease of life every few minutes. This discontinuity that is latent in continuity might be called the tell-tale heart of *Une Vie* – if only to show how close is the link between this supposedly cold film and the true master of mystery, Edgar Allan Poe, the most abstract author of all.

Just like *Bitter Victory*, *Une Vie* is a wonderfully simple film. But simplification does not mean stylisation. Astruc is here very different from Visconti, and it would be pointless to compare the two directors. In *Le Notti Bianche*, Maria Schell was certainly more efficiently used. But in *Une Vie* she is used in a better, more profound way. In his own time, Maupassant was, I suppose, a modern writer. Paradoxically, then, the best way to capture a genuine nineteenth-century atmosphere was to give the whole film an undisguisedly 1958 tone. Astruc and Laudenbach have succeeded magnificently. The only proof I need is the admirable answer that the admirable Christian Marquand gives to the woman who has offered him her dowry and her château: 'Because of you, I have ruined my life.' And another example: Marquand's bearing as he

83

carries Maria Schell in his arms seems just as modern as Jean-Claude Pascal's similar treatment of Anouk Aimée seemed old fashioned (in *Les Mauvaises Rencontres*).

When one has heaped all the praise one can on Pascale Petit (Astruc went to work on her in just as phenomenal a way as did Renoir on Françoise Arnoul in *French Cancan*) who runs through the undergrowth as deftly as Orvet and hides beneath the sheets better than Vadim's girls, all will not have been said. The title of *Une Vie* might well have been 'On the Threshold of the Unknown', with all its overtones of science fiction. For *Une Vie* forces the cinema to turn its gaze in another direction.

As I have said, what is remarkable in Godard's critical writing is the way it reflects Godard's cinematic thought and anticipates his own films. With Truffaut, there is less consistency of critical and creative attitudes. Less opinionated and more self-critical than Godard, he found the transition from the desire to make films to the actual realisation of this desire a much more complicated process. In this second extract from his interview of 1962, Truffaut, the most engaging and modest of the Cahiers *directors, discusses this problem at length, suggests why certain films failed, and talks about the influence of the American cinema on the Nouvelle Vague.*

7: Interview with François Truffaut (second extract)

And what about those films which, rightly or wrongly, are labelled as 'unreleasable'?

All those films have ended up by being released, one after the other. The success of 1959 went to people's heads, and some of them went a bit too far. I don't think a film should try to be new in every aspect. Perhaps a film by a new director needs something which keeps it anchored to the traditional cinema – a simple or strong subject, the presence of a star, or something like that. One feels that a lot of people have made their films without a thought in their head. In those of them which didn't do well, there is visibly too great a gulf between the director's ambitions and the result.

In 1955, I wrote an article in *Arts* in which I said that the crisis of French cinema (which was very real at the time) boiled down to a crisis of aspirations. I wrote: there are seven directors in France who aim to make a good film (which could, for example, be in line for the Prix Louis Delluc); twenty don't really give a damn; thirty-five only think of money but do a more or less honest job; and lastly, there are fifty who are utterly deplorable. How could ambition be stimulated? There had to be greater competition between films. And this is what happened in the end, beyond all one's expectations.

Let's take a look at some of the Nouvelle Vague films which have not been a success. There are those that are excellent but which go completely over people's heads; those that are no more than interesting; and then there are the failures. As far as the last category is concerned, there's only one thing to be done, which is pan them. That's normal enough. The problem comes when one tackles the films which are interesting but not well made. They all have one point in common: the scenario does not mean the same thing to the director as it does to the public. In this case, the faults probably arise from excessive self-confidence on the part of the director; or it may be that he has adapted a type of subject which requires something more than mere sincerity. Some subjects permit one to speak from the heart; what one has to say is so simple that no one can fail to understand. There are no problems here. Other subjects, however, pose problems which need thinking out. Problems of construction, for example. The camera has to shift from one character to another, it moves around, and that's where craftsmanship comes in. When one's in a particular place, one must be able to recognise it. The director is sometimes quite certain the audience can recognise the flat which the characters left half an hour previously, whereas the audience may well not recognise it at all. That side of film-making is important too.

For the sake of argument, let's divide films into two categories: those that are completely personal and reflect the state of mind of the artist when he shot it (*A Bout de Souffle*, for instance, which in my opinion is above all a kind of cry); and those that are shot in a cool and calculated manner, that are manufactured objects and should therefore be manufactured as well as possible. For example, all films of the detective-story type have to be well constructed. There are several ways of going about them. I feel that Paviot's *Portrait Robot*, Doniol-Valcroze's *La Dénonciation*, and Chabrol's *L'Oeil du Malin*, would all have gained from being discussed before shooting, perhaps in collaboration with somebody like Kast, who has a clear logical mind, or with a scriptwriter like Moussy. There can be no doubt that although all three of them are interesting films, the audience does not grasp exactly what the director wanted to say.

All in all, I don't think all that many films have been given an unfair deal. As far as I'm concerned, I have had only one misunderstanding with the public, *Tirez sur le Pianiste*, and I consider myself entirely responsible. And that, quite apart from the fact that the film was released in a manner that didn't correspond very well with its type.

You just mentioned one of your articles. How do you see your former position as a critic now?

My line in *Arts* was the same as it was in *Cahiers du Cinéma*. Especially at the start, for later I went in a rather more personal direction, as I had to discuss films which did not interest *Cahiers*. I also learnt to comply with certain requirements. In *Cahiers*, one doesn't have to tell the story of a film, but in a weekly paper one has to and this was a good exercise for me. Before then, I hardly even saw the films. I was so intoxicated by the cinema that I saw only movement and rhythm. Well, I had to force myself to consult a synopsis (at the beginning anyway), as I found it rather difficult to sum up a story. That brought home to me all the faults of certain scenarios, certain conventional narrative principles and techniques. This rich period was the equivalent for me, I suppose, of the training of a scriptwriter. It led me to see more clearly and evolve my tastes, my predilections, my biases. I came to dissect films so much that during my last year on *Arts* I was no longer writing criticism proper, I was speaking as a director. I used to get worked up only about what resembled what I wanted to do myself, and often I became too carried away and too nasty. Inversely, I still have something of the attitude of a critic. So when I finish a script, I feel I know, well perhaps not its faults, but at least what risks there are of being conventional and cliché-ridden. This guides me and gives me a kind of protection against this danger during shooting.

Each film presents different pitfalls. In *Les Quatre Cents Coups* it was the poetry of childhood; in *Tirez sur le Pianiste*, the attractiveness of someone who always proves other people wrong; in *Jules et Jim*, the character of the woman who could have become a first-class self-willed bitch. It so happens that by striving to avoid these pitfalls I made all three films sadder than I had planned. If you read the original script of *Les Quatre Cent Coups*, you will be surprised to

Les Quatre Cents Coups

find the framework of a comedy. In *Tirez sur le Pianiste*, where the danger was having a character who was too moving, I emphasised the egotistical side of the artist, his desire to cut himself off from the world, and his cowardice, so much so that he ends up rather unattractive, very hard and almost antipathetic. That may even be one of the reasons why the film failed. The same thing nearly happened with *Jules et Jim*; I didn't want the character played by Jeanne Moreau to be entirely sympathetic and I made her a little too hard.

When you made Les Quatrè Cents Coups, *did you worry a lot about this sort of problem?*

I made the film in a very instinctive way. The subject predominated. Such and such a scene had to be seen through the eyes of the boy, and so had to be shot in a certain way. Moreover, the film had a documentary side to it, and that required a good deal of neutrality. In fact, the people who were disappointed by *Les Quatre Cents Coups* were the *cinéphiles*. Over and above what a film expresses,

88

Tirez sur le Pianiste

they feel the need to find a *form* which arouses them like a stimulant. Well, the film had no such form, it was neutral; the direction was purely moral, self-effacing. When I see it again now, I also find it rather awkward, but the required effects were often very simple ones and it's a film which makes me feel very nostalgic. I get the feeling I'll never again find such a direct subject. There were things in it about which I felt so deeply that I had no choice, there was only one way to shoot them. What's more, now that I tend to produce more refined work (I am not using the word in a flattering sense, in fact I don't find it a step forward), I yearn for simple effects which are able to move everyone at the same time – I am very sensitive to the collective spectacle.

As for *mise-en-scène*, I first became really conscious of it from *Tirez sur le Pianiste* onwards. At the same time I wished I hadn't chosen such a flimsy story, so I tried to enjoy myself a bit.

Basically, there was the same principle in my criticism as there is in my direction. People say my films have nothing to do with what

Le Journal d'un Curé de Campagne

I used to write. Nothing could be further from the truth. I have the reputation of shortening my films a lot just before they come out, and then shortening them again between their first run and their general release. When I wrote an article, I often cut a third of it before taking it along to *Arts* as I was haunted by the idea of being a bore. I sometimes went so far as to replace long words by short ones. First of all I wrote rapidly, in a flurry, then I cut every third sentence to make it flowing and readable.

I always thought of the director while writing my article. I wanted to influence him (but when I attacked him, my way of influencing him could become very offensive). Above all, I wanted to convince him. I used to say to myself: 'This word will convince him more than that one.' That's also why my last year on *Arts* was less valuable. I would forget about the script the director had filmed and end up by suggesting the one he *ought* to have filmed.

But my tastes have not changed very much since then. I read recently: 'By having constant recourse to a commentary off, Truf-

Et Dieu Créa la Femme

faut the director is betraying his theories, etc.' In fact, I adored *Le Journal d'un Curé de Campagne*, *Les Enfants Terribles*, and *Le Plaisir*, and my criticism of Aurenche and Bost's adaptations was precisely that they were bad theatre, whereas it would have been more worthwhile to read a text out loud. This solution has always seemed better to me, when the interest of a book lies in its prose.

Now that you're a film-maker, don't you look at things differently?

I certainly don't make judgements in the same way. If I had to go back to film criticism, I would produce something different, but for another reason. The kind of cinema I used to champion is now with us. And now I can see its drawbacks (for it was inevitable that there would be some). Often people quote at me some of the things I wrote and that embarrasses me a lot. In *Arts*, I wrote, during a festival and without quite having recovered from the euphoria of *Et Dieu Créa la Femme* . . . : 'From now on, films no longer need to tell stories, it is enough to describe one's first love-affair, to take one's camera on to the beach', and so on. All that has become such cliché nowadays that it pains me a lot when what I wrote is quoted in connection with the cinema today. On the contrary, scriptwriting has been so maltreated since then that I now feel like seeing well-told stories. Of course, one shouldn't come to the conclusion that we should at all costs revert to the good old days of cinema.

I made *Jules et Jim* almost as a reaction against slipshod scenarios. I was told, for example, that I ought to have transposed the period of the book and brought it up to date. Everything could have fitted very nicely into the context of the Second World War. But as I was tackling the problems of women and love, I didn't want my film to fall into that category of film which is so prevalent nowadays, with a sports car (I would have needed one for the bridge sequence), whisky for the rendezvous, and, of course, the gramophone for a bit of music. I would have churned out a perfect piece of 'new cinema'. Through the solution I adopted – faithfulness to the book – I hoped to give *Jules et Jim* the atmosphere of one of those little films that MGM used to produce twenty or twenty-five years ago: *Mrs Parkington*, *The Green Years*, etc., films whose only fault was that they were conventional, but which *did* give the impression of a fat 800-page book, with the years rolling by and people's hair going grey. I didn't want to follow a fashion, even a fashion that has resulted in films I like, such as Kast's, for instance.

Are you someone who likes to make films for their own sake, without thinking of your audience?

No, I could never summon up enough enthusiasm to make films just for myself. I wouldn't make films if they weren't going to be seen. I have to feel I am producing a piece of entertainment. I could never write a novel, it's too abstract for me. I would prefer to advise singers on how to present their songs, to direct them, or else quite simply put on a music-hall show. When I do a job, I prefer it to be collective, and I must feel that the public is there to judge it. I have been asked to produce a play on the radio. This interests me, as the problem of voices is fascinating. But I shall try something that hasn't been done very often before: while the actors are playing, there will be thirty people in the studio who will act as an audience. I hope their reactions will help the actors.

Nor could I make a film if I knew it was automatically bound to be a success. My films are gambles. For me, shooting a film is like laying a bet. People took a strong dislike to the script of *Jules et Jim*. Distributors said: the woman is a tart; the husband will be grotesque, and so on. The gamble, for me, was to make the woman moving (without being melodramatic) and not a tart, and to prevent the husband from seeming ridiculous. I like to try to obtain something which isn't obvious at first sight. The same was true of *Les Quatre Cents Coups*. But there the problem was a false one, as the bet was won in advance. Only, I didn't realise this, and began the film more ingenuously than one could imagine. The gamble was to make people accept a boy who does a bit of thieving every five minutes. I was told: 'But you're mad. The boy will be antipathetic. People won't stand for it.' During the shooting, people were particularly surprised to see a kid pinching things left, right and centre. It looked as though I was doing a documentary on juvenile delinquents. I did take some notice of these warnings, and now wish I hadn't. In fact, neither myself nor my friends knew that an audience will forgive a child for anything and that it's always the parents who get the blame. I was wrong in thinking I was striking a balance. I was very naïve, but the film turned out to be naïvely rather subtle. Now, four years later, I can see that it's Hitchcockian. Why? Because from the first shot to the last, one identifies with the boy. At the time it was made, a lot of praise was heaped upon a silly film by Robert Montgomery: *The Lady in the Lake*, in which the whole film is seen through the eyes of one person. But a subjective camera is the negation of subjective cinema. When it replaces a character, one cannot identify oneself with him. The cinema becomes subjective when the actor's gaze meets that of the audience. And so if the audience feels the need to identify (even in a film where the director has no such intention), it automatically does so with the face whose gaze it meets most frequently during the film, with the actor who is most often shot full on and in close-up. This is what happened with

Jean-Pierre Léaud. I thought I was being objective, doing a documentary on him. But the more I shot him from the front, the more he gained in presence and the more the audience *became* him. I realised this when watching the film in public: I heard people scream (the sort of reaction they have when watching a film by Hitchcock) as soon as the mother appeared behind the window-panes of the classroom. It's true that as the scene was a difficult one I gave it a lot of preparation, instead of improvising as I often did on set; but the anxiety arises from the fact that the spectators sense that the child is particularly concerned (and all the more so as they feel very sympathetic towards him when he says his mother is dead). So it was a totally naïve film, which I shot without knowing the first thing about the rules of film-making. At the same time, it was unwittingly subtle, much more than what I have made since.

In a sense, I made *Tirez sur le Pianiste* as a reaction against *Les Quatre Cents Coups*. For with the success of the latter film came the sudden realisation of its unevenness; and this worried me so much that I told myself to be careful never to play down to my audience. But I don't quite realise what happened with *Tirez sur le Pianiste*. It must have been that I was too faithful to the book. I was also too sure of myself because *Les Quatre Cents Coups* had been such a success. But I also feel that as a general rule one's second film is worse than one's first. For instance, *Une Femme Est Une Femme* (as *Le Petit Soldat* was banned, I consider it to be Godard's second film) was made under the euphoric influence of *A Bout de Souffle*. *Vivre Sa Vie* marked Godard's regaining of control.

For one's first film, one takes the plunge: 'What the hell! I'm risking everything. Perhaps I'll never make films again, but while I can I want to see what I can do.' People's reaction to one's first film is very important. If it is a success one is always surprised. This affects one's second film. *Marienbad* reveals great self-confidence which arose from the unexpected success of *Hiroshima*. All these second films I mentioned have one thing in common: they are less complete than the first ones, where there was a whole beginning of life to express, where one wanted to say everything one had to say.

One's second film is voluntarily less ambitious in intent. The third one is the most interesting; it is a reflection of the first two and marks the start of a career.

When one thinks about *Tirez sur le Pianiste*, one can see that the scenario does not stand up to analysis. It clearly lacks the kind of guiding line one can find in my other two films. In *Les Quatre Cents Coups*, the idea was to show, as simply as possible, a boy being driven by certain moral prejudices. The same was true of *Jules et Jim*: done one way it would have been pornographic, another way coarse, another way conventional, and so I had to do it completely differently. The trouble with *Tirez sur le Pianiste* was that one could do it any way one wanted, there was a content which didn't require a particular form. Aznavour has a great comic talent, and I could have made a very funny film out of it. He also possesses great authority; I could have made a very imposing character out of him. At the start I had no particular ideas about this, I simply wanted madly to use Aznavour after his performance in *La Tête Contre les Murs*; but it would have been better if I had known him longer. What was courageous about *Tirez sur le Pianiste* was that I used flashbacks, while knowing very well that they can never go down well. I said to Braunberger: 'Do you remember *Les Mauvaises Rencontres*? And *Lola Montès*? And *The Barefoot Contessa*? They did not work out because of the flashbacks.' That's why the whole thing was ruined.

It is a rule: one should not mix things. One cannot be plumb in the middle of one story and plumb in the middle of another one too. With a bit of thought I certainly could have given *Tirez sur le Pianiste* a chronological narrative line. It just needed a bit of work. The film has *something*. But no one could say: 'It's the best that's been done on such and such a theme.' There is no theme.

Unless perhaps, it's this one: a man is caught up in a mechanism, tries to reject it, but ends up by resigning himself to it. Courage, cowardice. . . .

But even then there are superfluous things in it. And what about the director who resigned himself to being caught up in the mechanism of the gangster film? I had never thought about it before, but as I was shooting *Tirez sur le Pianiste* I realised I hated gangster films. I would never now write articles praising *Rififi*. I feel there is no point in making gangsters moving, in showing crooks weeping and pitting goodies against baddies. The film that results has all the *bourgeois* conventions simply transposed into the world of gangsters. That's why I suddenly decided to make my gangsters funny. It was the only solution if I was not to lapse into conventionalism. I rather made fun of them. To compensate for this, I also had to make them rather frightening, which I did through the kidnapping of the boy and the death of Marie Dubois. That brought people up with a start – they might otherwise have thought they were watching British cardboard characters. The only thing is, it is dangerous to change course during a film. One should have one idea at the beginning and reinforce it during the film, as I did in my other two films whose themes were originally expressed rather weakly in the scenario. If I'd known, beforehand, that Aznavour and Nicole Berger would make a wonderful couple (the others did not go together so well), I would have made a film about those two.

One thing which must have worried the public in Tirez sur le Pianiste *was the change of tone. This is a characteristic of several films which have not done well – including* Une Femme Est Une Femme *– and it is something the French public doesn't seem to be able to accept.*

Yes, that's the most difficult thing to make them swallow. Incidentally, in the USA they understood *Tirez sur le Pianiste*, but in a different way: they didn't stop laughing once, even during the most dramatic sequences. The first song was funny, so they laughed all through the second one, which wasn't supposed to be.

Anyway, say what you like, I'm still convinced that *Tirez sur le Pianiste* needed another month's work. Slap together two or three reels of film that appeal to you, and you won't necessarily make a film that appeals to other people, even if what's in them is good. It's also true that a change of tone is a thing which has to be carefully worked out; it's a gamble worth trying occasionally. Renoir has brought it off.

But La Règle du Jeu *was a failure with the public.*

96

Une Partie de Campagne

Yes, but *La Règle du Jeu* is one of the rare cases of a film which completely went over the heads of the public. In *Une Partie de Campagne*, on the other hand, there are some false changes of tone. The characters are very schematic. There is the fat one who makes people laugh, and the two little fops from Paris . . . why, it's pure Maupassant! There is an element of cautiousness about the film. The only reason the story does not become improper or smutty is because one isn't shown everything. Just suppose one really saw Brunius lying on Jane Marken, or imagine them getting dressed afterwards. The film consists of a selection, in a double love-story, of the moments which people are willing to see. It is true that sometimes an audience should be given a good shaking-up. I really think it's very important to please the public, but I also think that one should start out with the intention of premeditated assault. One should force people to watch something they are bound not to like, force them to approve of a character whom they hate or refuse to watch.

Roughly speaking, there is the belief that there are directors who think of their audience and there are those who don't. That's not quite true. There are those who think of their films as an entity which the audience is part of, and those who think only of that part of the spectacle which is the film. What does the cinema a lot of harm is the kind of idea people have of a person like Resnais. Resnais would never say: I think of my audience. Nor does he do so, strictly speaking. But he *does* consider his film as a spectacle, and I am quite sure that when he made *Marienbad* he thought of his audience's emotional reaction, of the line of his scenario, of its balance – for otherwise there would have been no reason for not making *Marienbad* last eight hours. Resnais is not Stroheim, his films last an hour and a half, and they are composed in a very studied fashion.

Well, some young people see Resnais's films as an example of courage instead of an example of skill. It all began with *Hiroshima*. They said: 'Resnais is wonderful, he has proved that anything is possible.' Not at all. All that's proved is that anything is possible for *Resnais*. At first sight, in *Hiroshima*, there was everything there should not have been: the combination of adultery and the atomic bomb, of a general problem and a very particular one, of a social and a political problem, and within its political aspect, the mixture of a big problem – the bomb – with a smaller one, the scandal of reprisals after the Liberation. That was like mixing oil and water. And so it was an extraordinary achievement to have got it across. But it doesn't mean one should try to repeat what only Resnais could bring off.

A lot of films were made by people who admired the artistic freedom of *Hiroshima*. It was thought that there was no need for a subject any more, no need to think of the public. But Resnais *did* think of them. He knew very well that by making Riva do this or that he would generate a particular emotion in the cinema. The naïve film-maker is encouraged instead of discouraged by *Hiroshima*. I don't mean that *Hiroshima* should necessarily act as a discouragement, but that one should realise the skill of the man who managed to bring it off, and not think: 'That's fine, I can do that too.' I think

Resnais would help people if he emphasised the difficulties he encountered, instead of giving them the impression that they should make anything that comes into their head.

It remains to be seen why it was that certain films, such as *Une Femme Est Une Femme*, didn't get across to the public. As far as this film is concerned, I would say that one can reach one's audience in almost any conceivable way, but not by assaulting their basic peace of mind. If one plays around with the sound-track and the images in too unusual a way, people start objecting – it is a normal reaction. They ripped up the seats at Nice because they thought the projection box was not properly equipped. Of course one could explain things to people through articles, but in those cinemas where the film was put on the audiences were taken by surprise. Godard went too far for them in the sound-mixing. When the girl comes out of the café, there's suddenly no sound, just complete silence. Straight away people think the projector has broken down. Although, of course, those spectators in Nice were not civilised – one simply does not knife cinema seats.

A similar case was *Lola Montès*. This film offered a striking paradox: it was an *avant-garde* film shot within the framework of the commercial cinema. Moreover, when one re-sees *La Ronde* in the light of *Lola Montès*, one can see that Ophuls came very close to disaster – *La Ronde* was very coolly received at its première at the Opéra: there was no story, and one could sense an enormous gulf between the author and his characters. At that time, people expected Ophuls to produce something of the Christian-Jaque type.

Another factor involved in *Une Femme Est Une Femme* is the originality of the film: it breaks all the rules of its genre. People expected to see a nice little classical story: a girl and two men in Paris. . . . The very story line, in fact, that one expects to be told in a classical way. They were flabbergasted. Just imagine *Marienbad* with the same sound-mixing. No one would have batted an eyelid. Whereas here people expected to see one thing, and they were given something else. This didn't make them at all happy. What was needed was the kind of label *Marienbad* got, to the effect that it was a strange film that didn't fit into any category.

Une Femme est une Femme

In *Une Vie*, one would have thought there was plenty to please the public: Maupassant, colour, Maria Schell, and so on. But the story didn't correspond to the title, and the film was subtly turned against Maria Schell, whereas people came with the expectation of liking her. There too, what they were led to expect and what they got were two entirely different things.

I have also wondered about this problem in relation to my own films. I thought the title of *Les Quatre Cents Coups* suggested a lot of things which were not all in the film, and people were going to feel cheated. But they didn't, perhaps because the scenes were short and there were a lot of them. As for *Jules et Jim*, I thought that two men's names as the title of a film chiefly about a woman sounded a bit funny. But they accepted it.

Les Bonnes Femmes seems to me to have failed for the same reasons as *Lola Montès*: it comes too close to the theatre of derision. That was Beckett's influence. There is a good theme to be found in girls who are destined to die, but when one shows working-class people

such as shop-girls, the audience expects something realistic, dramatic, or psychological – in fact, anything but what they got.

The success of the 'unusual' Nouvelle Vague films was due to the
fact that they were totally unusual and were labelled as such; people
came to see them as curiosities. Resnais, who is considered a specialist in all that is unusual and so to speak holds the patent for it
(that doesn't make me think any the less of him), has the right to do
this sort of thing. But if one day he consented to make a 'normal'
film, there would be serious consequences for him.

As for *Lola*, it probably failed because of the post-synchronisa-
tion. I know Rivette doesn't agree with me, and has told me in no
uncertain terms that he feels it was just what was needed and that
Demy wanted to make the voices tend towards song. Okay, but in
La Baie des Anges at any rate, Demy took a hell of a lot of trouble
over the direct sound-track.

People don't mind a realistic story becoming melodramatic, but they do
mind a film that starts as melodrama and ends up by going beyond it.

That's probably true, but it's just what Demy likes to produce:
over-melodramatic melodrama. This is perhaps the result of his
almost perverse sense of refinement. All the same, I was moved, and
I think the general public was too.

There's one phenomenon especially which is making things difficult at the moment. The attitude of the Parisian critics and *cinéphiles*
is openly hostile to the difficult film. When films used to be vulgar
and play down to their audiences, they said what a disgrace it was
to treat people like fools. It would now seem that the critics, and
even the audiences of premières, are concerned most of all with
whether a film is going to make a profit. For a film to run the risk
of losing money is shameful in their eyes. This attitude is especially
noticeable in the critics of the dailies. The idea of helping a film's
career used to appeal to them, but now they think that out of date.
The paradoxical result of this is that the initiated and educated
public, as well as the critics, have become more hostile to difficult
films than the industry is. At the première of *Eve*, Losey was blamed
most of all for having made a film which courted disaster at the box-

office. What happened was that everyone expected things to change, and now that they have, everyone is irritated if the product is too specialised. Nowadays, people have even turned their spite on Antonioni (whom, by the way, I don't like). There was delirium about two of his films, and now people are giving him a good working over. This had happened to Bergman and is now happening to Losey. It all starts in Paris, but everyone else follows suit. It's all the more unfortunate for Bergman, as his last film, *The Silence*, is a good deal better than the preceding ones.

What amuses me is the way people get hot under the collar about private jokes or winks at the audience. It's quite simple: when we started we were so happy to be making films, and films before then had been such solemn affairs, that it seemed wonderful to be able to make a few jokes. I found it was an amusing way of personalising a product which up to then had been awfully impersonal. In fact, this didn't irritate our friends, nor those who weren't aware of what was going on, but simply the friends of our friends. The critic Charensol said to himself: 'I saw eight private jokes in that film, so there must have been at least fifteen,' and he got annoyed at the idea of the seven he had failed to catch. If a private joke replaced something important, then of course someone who couldn't understand would feel out of it, and it would be a stupid device. But when it's added after everything else, why should anyone worry? Say one has a character called Tartempion; one might as well call him Delannoy or Domarchi, if that gives it a double meaning. But this is where the initiated public starts objecting, for they decide to identify themselves with the general provincial public. Whereas the latter doesn't mind at all, and with good reason.

One shouldn't let the audiences of first-run cinemas lay down the law. In the last account, they are a public neither of film-lovers nor of ordinary people. Film-enthusiasts love *Marienbad*, popular audiences love *Ben Hur*. The audiences of first-run cinemas yawn during both of them and don't even know why.

There's another new element. Nowadays, everyone talks in figures. So-and-so says such and such a film had 167,273 admissions. What the hell has that got to do with it? When I was on *Cahiers*, I would never have mentioned such figures in an article. I think the fashion for statistics came in with the Nouvelle Vague. People tried to make comparisons: did *Les Cousins* do better than one of Clément's films, etc. If one is going to talk figures, one should be thorough about it. Then one can see that many films which don't do very well in France more than make up for it abroad. On the other hand, films scripted by Audiard hardly ever leave French-speaking countries. There's the difficulty of dubbing dialogue which, once translated, no longer stands up to examination. What's more, Gabin doesn't mean very much abroad. Whence the desperate device of *Un Singe en Hiver*, where Belmondo was stuck in with Gabin so that the film could be sold abroad.

But don't let's lose our heads. We must persevere. Okay, we are living in a capitalist system, so let's use the weapons at our disposal, let's shuffle the cards. Look at the case of Godard. In one sense, he is marginal to the general body of the film industry; and yet he could, if he wanted to, find a way of integrating himself into the system. His is a case apart. He's interested in making a mixture of everything: the moment his story becomes fictional, he becomes Rouch-like, and then he suddenly goes off in another direction. But his career has been very logical. Look at the articles he wrote in *Cahiers*. From the beginning, he always displayed a kind of disdain for total fiction. He always liked films in which the subject was destroyed. But his temperament is so strong that one cannot question what he does. He does it in a certain way and he's right.

What does the American cinema mean for you, now that you're a director?

In comparison with American directors, I think we are all intellectuals – even myself, who am less so than the others. One shouldn't cheat; one shouldn't pretend to be unsophisticated or ingenuous when one's thinking about a script or putting the final touches to it. One shouldn't force oneself. That's probably where Melville is wrong, in imitating the brutality and uncouthness of the Americans. But as long as one considers the cinema as a popular art – and we all do as we were brought up on the American cinema – then we can go off on another tack: we can discipline our work so that it becomes complex and has more than one layer of meaning. It's the same principle as the three films superimposed on each other that Hitchcock produces. He is one of the few film-makers who appeals to everyone, so he's a good example to follow. I believe that we can apply his principle. To be more precise, this is only worthwhile when one works a film out carefully. Resnais elaborates a lot. I don't think you will find *effective* devices or emotions in *Marienbad* which cannot also be found in *Vertigo*. I maintain that Resnais was absolutely right to make *Marienbad*. But if one is not Resnais, if one doesn't possess that extraordinary control which he has over what he is working on, one will do better to be less ambitious. Not that one should limit one's ambitions; one should simply be modest in the way one achieves them, one should make films whose appearance is unpretentious. I don't think the world needs my films, I don't think the world needs me; I feel rather that I must get myself accepted by it, and that the way to do this is by my work.

Nowadays it's said that people no longer go to the cinema in a haphazard manner, they go to see what they have heard about. We should honestly find out if this selective public is large enough to render a film that costs £50,000 profit-earning, and whether it might not be advisable also to reckon on those who are not selective. Such a film, in order to break even, must make at least £250,000 at the box-office. One should work out how many admissions that means at 3s 6d per seat. One would have to include people who come in by chance or through habit. Can one afford to forget about them? And so the inevitable conclusion is that *Les Bonnes Femmes*, for instance, needs to be seen by people who are exactly like the characters of the film: shop-girls, who have come to the cinema instead of going dancing. Well, people who see themselves in a film can't see themselves in perspective; they can't understand the film – its intention is abstract and, what's more, partly based on a derisive attitude. It transcends mere derision, it's more profound than that, that's why I like it – but people can't grasp that.

It's at this point that one might imagine another way of making the film than the one Chabrol adopted, which was almost too pure

Les Bonnes Femmes (above and opposite)

and confidential. The same film, saying the same things, could have had a second story: the story of the murder, that of Weidmann. Instead of coming as a finale, the crime could have acted as a kind of suspense which would have gripped everybody while still allowing Chabrol to say what he wanted to say. What if we tried for a moment to imagine how Hitchcock would go about a film like *Les Bonnes Femmes*. First of all, he would choose an extremely simple title, something like *The Shop-girl Vanishes*. The film begins. One fine morning, the first shop-girl doesn't turn up at the shop; she is not at home either, she has simply disappeared into thin air. Surprise. When Hitchcock gets to the second girl, he will own up and show us the young woman being strangled by the motor-cyclist. Horror. As for the third girl, there would be pure suspense; the audience *knows* that the motor-cyclist is a killer, but the girl does not. A short lovers' walk through the forest, a bit of love-making in idyllic surroundings; then the works. Finally we get to the fourth girl who, of course, will be saved just in time, by her fiancé

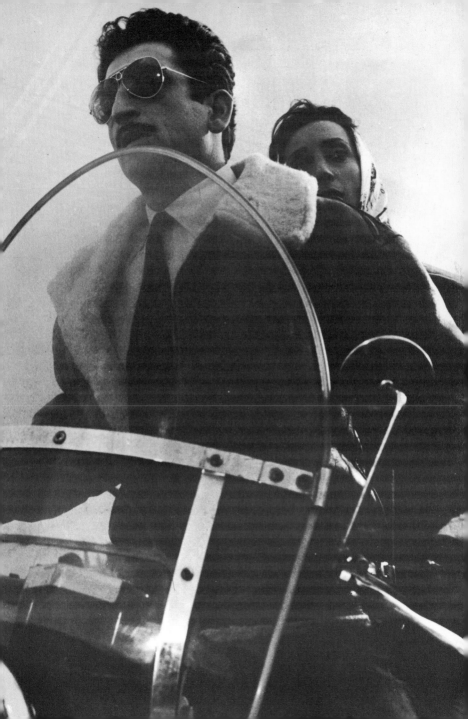

probably, and the criminal will end up nicely mangled by his own motor-bike.

Don't tell me it would be inferior or vulgar done that way. Just think of *Shadow of a Doubt* and Uncle Charlie's thoughts: the world is a pigsty, and honest people like bankers and widows detest the purity of virgins. It's all there, but inserted into a framework which keeps you on the edge of your seat. *Les Bonnes Femmes* is a calculated, well thought out, cerebral film. So why not make the extra effort which would have consisted of telling the story in entertainment terms, then superimpose on to this basic layer of the film a second and even a third layer? Even so, it remains, for me, Chabrol's best film.

I think above all in entertainment terms – music-hall, variety – but I also have preoccupations which are not shared by the majority of my audience. The problem of *Jules et Jim*, for instance, doesn't interest all that many people. What's more, nine out of every ten people who see the film consider divorce shocking. To ask these people to sympathise with a couple of layabouts who never do an honest day's work and live with the same woman is tantamount to an insult. So I have to give them something instead, emotion for example, as when the characters push themselves to their very limits; I am thinking of the weeping scene (which was improvised) between Werner and Jeanne Moreau. I don't want people to come out of the cinema saying 'This is scandalous.' I would be the first to be pained by this. Of course, it's impossible to satisfy everyone, but it *is* possible not to ruin their evening entirely. If they come out saying 'Luckily there was that song', or 'Luckily there were some nice shots of the countryside', or 'Luckily there were some war newsreels', well, that's something, and it's better than nothing.

One has to know exactly what one wants to obtain, and, above all, one shouldn't try to obtain more than one thing at a time. The idea is to create emotions. So, before each film, each scene, each shot, we pause a moment and ask ourselves how we are going to create this emotion. Everything that comes into the film, the scene, or the shot, which doesn't answer this question becomes a parasitic element which should be rejected. We are working in a medium that is both

Truffaut directing *Jules et Jim*

literary, musical, and visual; everything must always be simplified as much as possible. A film is a boat which is always on the point of sinking – it always tends to break up as you go along and drag you under with it. And if one pays no attention to this fact, then one's had it. In our job, one should never consider oneself indispensable. In one respect, the Americans are infuriating: if a good film has been a failure at the box-office, they are ashamed of it. That's going too far. In another respect, they do have a healthy 'show business' side to them. One doesn't come across people in Hollywood who think that all is due to them and say it's a disgrace they didn't receive such and such a prize or subsidy. The French attitude is that all films should be subsidised, whatever they eventually turn out to be like. In short, people want the advantages of both the capitalist and socialist systems.

The massive arrival of the Nouvelle Vague directors has created a lot of competition and has made the system tend to become more like that of Hollywood. It has become more difficult to escape from a given category, or to recover from a failure. As things stand at the moment, it's better to have made no films at all rather than to have just made one which was a flop.

Orson Welles, who has never been commercial, commands such respect and admiration, and has such prestige, that every four years or so he manages to make something like *The Trial*. Someone puts their faith in him and the fifteen greatest actors in Europe are delighted to shoot with him. That's all very fine. Perhaps Resnais will reach the same position one day. In the long run, there is a kind of justice. People said to Raoul Lévy: 'Why don't you take Orson Welles to direct *Marco Polo*?' 'Who? Welles? Why, he's through, he's no good any more.' And now Raoul Lévy is beseeching him to agree to finish off the *Marco Polo* which Christian-Jaque started.

You mentioned a kind of justice. Aren't you taking for granted that there are producers willing to accept risks?

Yes, but the mistake producers made was to take too long to get used to the idea that it's the director who *makes* a film, and that a film will never be worth more than its director. Once they had got this into their heads, they should never, of course, have given a difficult film to a director who had been used to commercial film-making, nor vice versa. The results can be absurd. A balance must be struck. The Hollywood system was balanced. And it's amazing to watch the terrible way Hollywood declined as soon as the traditional structure broke up. Everything went well when films were the result of a production line, when the director had no say in the matter, when scriptwriters were paid a yearly salary, when films were edited by specialists who had no contact with the director, and so on. The moment the chains were loosened, the whole thing collapsed. In another domain, there's nothing worse than half-baked Hollywood cinema. For instance, things are going badly in Germany at the moment. There is Madame Kubachewsky who gives strict orders about the way a good film must be made: there must be nice characters, flocks and pastures, children's choirs, fine clothes,

and a happy ending 'even if it's completely unexpected'. When people swallow all this advice, the result is the 'Sissi' series, which has managed to prove itself, but whose posters look as though they were advertising Camembert rather than a film. And now even Madame Kubachewsky is having trouble.

The Americans had one inimitable quality: in every department they knew how to give life to what they were working on. And the scripts were often admirable pieces of work. I have just received a scenario by Philip Yordan. Everything is there, including the humour; there's no need to change a line, one could just go out and shoot it. Basically the American cinema consisted of the best and the worst. It was usually happier when dealing with traditional subjects, but as long as it did so the results were brilliant.

Lastly, not everybody deserves to be given total freedom. A lot of new film-makers aren't mature enough and they really do make too many blunders. Most of the films I see are poorly edited. Because of self-satisfaction, lack of critical acumen, and laziness, their directors are unwilling to make cuts. Once upon a time I laughed at Becker when he said: 'The cinema is very complicated.' Temperamentally, I was on the side of those who said it was simple. But it's a luxury to say that, and not everyone can afford to. There are some very plucky people who produce their own films, and do everything themselves, even though this means getting over a mountain of difficulties. But in the last account, it's not in their interest to do everything themselves; it ceases to be a question of courage, but becomes ignorance or carelessness.

When one has a good look round, one can see that there's no really good producer or scriptwriter in France. And so one finds oneself terribly alone to face one's responsibilities, much more alone than an American director. We have to have some of the qualities which go to make both a good director and a good scriptwriter, as there is no room in the French system for the film director pure and simple.

One should also begin to think about television as a new vehicle. It's a medium of expression which has advantages as well as shortcomings. The other evening there was a play which was badly directed but very well acted by three elderly actresses. In the cinema, it would have been a total disaster. No one would have gone out of their way to see it. And yet it has been one of the better programmes on television this year. When one comes across a subject of that kind and one wants very much to direct it, one should shoot it on a very low budget for television, I feel.

In another respect, television uses a lot of long-held shots, and almost never comes off when cross-cutting is used. And so as a reaction it's a good idea in the cinema to revert to a classical breakdown of shots and chop them up a lot. Five years ago, when I was a critic, I found all French films ugly. That is why the first films of Vadim and Malle were important, simply because they displayed a basic minimum of taste; nowadays, everyone has taste, and films are tidier on the whole. So one should aim at something higher, at something beautiful, intelligent, clear, moving, interesting. In other words, as Ingmar Bergman put it, we should make very one of our films 'as though it were our last', we should force ourselves to make progress.

The critics of Positif *had always delighted in crossing swords with* Cahiers *critics on questions of critical ideology. How did they react to their films? In this second extract from his article 'In Praise of André Bazin', Gérard Gozlan goes on to discuss,* en passant, *some of the films made by* Cahiers *directors and give a lengthy and detailed criticism of Jacques Rivette's* Paris Nous Appartient.

8: In praise of André Bazin (second extract)

Gérard Gozlan

Since the Nouvelle Vague is itself reluctant to define itself, it is difficult and presumptuous at this point to group certain new film-makers under a single heading. However, in order to make analysis feasible, it is, I think, possible (partly because of a common background of film criticism which first enabled some kind of definition and because of a catchphrase which they helped to spread) to limit the term Nouvelle Vague to the *Cahiers* group and a few film-makers whose 'moral and metaphysical outlook' is fairly close to that of the group. But this is only a verbal designation which will make discussion more convenient. For in fact, while we on *Positif* feel that it is not easy as yet to put one's finger on the way in which Jacques Demy, Jacques Doniol-Valcroze, and Claude de Givray resemble, in what they have directed, Godard, Rivette, or Chabrol, we are quite certain that Godard, Rivette, and Chabrol have common preoccupations. But where are we to put Kast? Astruc? Rozier? Clearly this can be only a working hypothesis. Once we accept it, then it is quite apparent that André Bazin's system has a lot of links with the Nouvelle Vague as defined in this way. And in case anyone doubts the importance of the role Bazin played in the practical training of the Nouvelle Vague, let us confront the latter with some of the governing ideas of the system.

For this confrontation, we could choose any Nouvelle Vague film, or almost any: *Le Beau Serge*, in which sacrifice, renunciation, and guilt vie with each other for the chief place, and the communion of

Jules et Jim

human beings is lumped together with Brialy's horrible tubercular cough; a very overrated *A Bout de Souffle*, a very odd *Petit Soldat*, or that episode in *Les Sept Péchés Capitaux* (*Sloth*) in which Godard extends the boundaries of nonchalant insignificance and proves once and for all that one should shut up when one has nothing to say; *Le Signe du Lion*, which bursts at the seams with muddled thinking; *Cartouche*, quite a pleasant film, but marred by an exasperating cult of the hero. I will not linger over the conclusion of *Jules et Jim* (the ridiculous aspect of our ashes is supposed to prove that our existences are ridiculous too); and the suffocated naturalism of *Les Bonnes Femmes*.

We are not of the opinion, however, that everything produced by the Nouvelle Vague has been nasty, stupid, or uninteresting. We do not believe that a large group of directors can all be categorised together or that they should be the objects of constant and unremitting

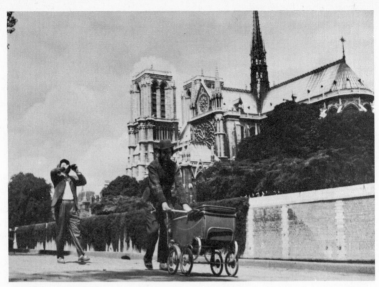

Le Signe du Lion

contempt. It is true after all that Chabrol now repudiates the mystic conclusion of *Le Beau Serge*. There is tenderness and humour in Truffaut: *Les Mistons* is a pleasant first film and *Tirez sur le Pianiste* is good Marcel Aymé. There are one or two good ideas in *A Bout de Souffle*, and some charming digressions in *Une Femme Est Une Femme*, a film that consists entirely of digression. No one can deny that the striking and morbid sensibility revealed by *Le Signe du Lion* and *Paris Nous Appartient* produces some fine moments. It is even possible that the Nouvelle Vague will one day produce masterpieces. But I would like to make one point: these masterpieces may well turn up eventually, but the Nouvelle Vague will only produce them by going against the drift of what it is trying to produce at the moment. In order to try and clarify this point, I have decided to take a close look at *Paris Nous Appartient*. More than any of the others quoted above, Rivette's film is the one I feel best represents the most ambitious side of the Nouvelle Vague: the desire to bear witness to our age.

Paris Nous Appartient: at the flat in Neuilly

As far as I have been able to fathom its extremely involved plot, which has certainly been affected by several successive versions of the script and re-editings which cut down its length, *Paris Nous Appartient* is a cryptic film full of bizarre characters. A certain De Georges, a doctor like Mabuse or Cordelier, seems to be rather powerful and to have few scruples. Pierre (François Maistre) does some rather shady work for him – at least that is what we are left to suppose, as he does not dare to talk about it to his nice, naïve younger sister, Anne (Betty Schneider). Others perhaps stand for 'the left'. At three one morning, for instance, in a flat in Neuilly, we get to know some individuals who are inspired by some subversive and anarchist spirit. They include: an anti-MacCarthyite who has been expelled from the USA, Philip Kaufman (Daniel Crohem); Terry (Françoise Prévost), a woman of means who supports needy artists; a nasty piece of work, Bernard (André Thorent), who has a rather uncharitable way of kicking Philip out and is able to parry awkward questions about the death of Mayakovsky. We should not overlook the charming young women who just talk, a couple of proud-looking Spaniards who recall 'their defeat', Rivette himself talking about 'crushed revolutions', finally the unspeakable Claude Chabrol, who talks a lot of stuff and nonsense, which, although left-wing rubbish, is none the less rubbish. The individuals of this select gathering, drunk and rude, glare at each other like china dogs and insult each other to a point where it gets embarrassing for them and the Revolution they are supposed to stand for. I say they represent the Revolution because they talk about it in hurried snatches, with facial expressions that are heavy with significance; but to tell the truth, we are here entering unknown country, and this lack of definition is part of the film's intended meaning. How did these people gathered together here first meet? What is their ideology? What are their tactics, their policy? When do they discuss? When do they act? What are their resources? Who assists them, what are their financial means? We never know, just as we never know anything about De Georges, except that he may be supposed to stand for the Forces of Money, that he likes *ingénues*, and that he is as enigmatic as Evil itself.

And so the situation described in *Paris Nous Appartient* can be taken as you want to take it; let's call it a 'fable', which aims, through its abstraction, at giving a synthetic account of most of all possible generalities. This is a method used extensively by Bazin. In fact, this 'possibly left-wing' get-together, of which we are given a general description, reminds one of nothing so much as the 'definitely right-wing' get-together which is so preposterously portrayed in *Les Cousins*. In the latter film, there may be less talk of politics, more loot and more chicks; the obsessions of the character played by Brialy are Nazi-like, but Bernard's hypocrisy is just as repulsive. Just as much is drunk, and what a good idea to make the characters of *Paris Nous Appartient* exclaim from time to time, as though illuminated by the Grace of God: 'We are all fools!', or else 'The whole world is in exile!' For it has to be drummed into people's heads that all is in all and vice versa. 'My film,' says Rivette, 'will be a film in which the strongest characters will behave in rather a cowardly way, the most intelligent will talk the most rubbish, and the most lucid will completely delude themselves' (interview in *Radio-Cinéma-TV*). This duality, which leads to a synthetic conception of the universe, is reconstituted by Rivette as follows: 'I have deeply experienced this search for truth via error which constitutes the main theme of the film. What do we see for more than two hours ? People who want to be able to explain the world to themselves through a single idea (the idea of a fascist organisation and conspiracy), who can't help deluding themselves and getting into terrible trouble. This doesn't mean that fascism doesn't exist; far from it, I would say that to a certain extent it stands for the Forces of Evil. What this does mean is that it is too easy to explain the world through a single idea. An idea can only exist because of a contrary idea, there must be a dialectic, etc.' (interview in *Les Lettres Françaises*, No. 905, December 1961). The guilty then are those who are taken in by 'the fascination of the schematism of a single solution. There lies the danger' (*ibid*). And Terry, who lets herself be taken in and shoots Pierre whom she mistakenly holds responsible for the death of Gérard* is clearly Rivette's mouthpiece when she learns the lesson from her mistake: 'It's so convenient to envelop everything, including one's inertia and cowardice, in a single idea. Evil has more than one face – that would be too easy.'

Of course it *may* be that Rivette wants to depict as thoroughly as possible an age in which the problems of living and understanding life have yet to be clearly defined – don't let's be ashamed to admit it. It *may* be that Rivette intended to allude to problems that would give us food for thought: on the one hand, the intelligent and stubborn resistance of capitalist and reactionary forces that are often still immature; and on the other hand, the problems faced by

---

*I have not introduced Gérard yet. He is the young theatre producer who wants very much to put on Shakespeare's *Pericles*; but as he has no backers he has to take his actors as they come. He is supported by Terry which visibly is not very much to his liking. One day he is asked to put *Pericles* on in a big Paris theatre: Terry has slept with an influential impresario. But in the end Gérard refuses to compromise. He stagnates for a time, then commits suicide, acting partly on a whim but much more in protest against his failure in the theatre.

Communist parties since the death of Lenin. The solution of these problems has led not only to the victory of socialism in one part of the world but also to the tragic mistakes which we may legitimately suppose not to have been inherent in a revolutionary state.

But then we want to see the goods. Well, *Paris Nous Appartient* does not keep its promises about the problems of this type that we would have liked to have seen treated. If Rivette found himself unable to solve them, he might at least have made an effort to pose them properly. But just look at Rivette's strange conception of fascism: 'To a certain extent it stands for the Forces of Evil.' We realise that the system of Bazin the master and the embellishments contributed by his disciples are rich in metaphysical *a priori* statements and journeys to the Heaven of pure religious Ideas. But all the same! It was not a bad idea of Rivette's to try to denounce the dangers of schematism, but the trouble with *Paris Nous Appartient* is that it is a film that is both extremely schematic and extremely confused. After all, a search for the truth via the false, if one's aim is *practical* truth, must consist of something more meaty than all that rushing about, 'doors being opened and closed, stairs mounted and descended, actions that turn out to be useless, a long effort in a labyrinth in order to depict the process of the truth' *(ibid)*. This assimilation of a search for the truth with a Journey to the centre of the earth clearly results in a curious conception of dialectics: 'the lack of a single solution', or, if you like, an ambiguity that renders the contradictory richness of reality, without our really being able to find out what this richness, this contradiction, or this reality consists of. For two hours, we follow the comings and goings of Anne Goupil. For Rivette, who follows her 'lovingly', she must, like Marina in *Pericles*, be the sign of Innocence metaphysically ensnared in the toils of society and politics, and buffeted on high seas by an unfavourable wind, a malicious wind, a crafty wind that the Holy Family is always breathing down our necks. Bazin and Bresson make no bones about saying that 'it blows where it will'. That crafty old fox, Jean-Jacques Gautier, is not all that far from the truth as Rivette conceives of it when he sees in Anne 'all that can remain of traditional purity and innocence, all that can be salvaged of eternal childhood in this "creature" ' (*Le Figaro*, November 1960). Anne shares with the great Saints the ability to safeguard all that is 'eternal' in each of us, in our troubled times where everything is going wrong, in a world where shadows spend their time running after each other: as total blackness is as significant as total whiteness, the total realism of the black screen is here offered us – it is, of course, not just any old realism, but one that is nourished by the shadows and half-shadows of reality, being in consequence the most realistic realism that exists. . . . Thus, like Groucho, who 'started out with a penny and ended up with nothing', *Paris Nous Appartient* starts out from nothing and ends up with *all*, or *nothing*, as you will. Jean-François Revel has put it in a nutshell: 'This film has deliberately been placed under the sign of ambiguity. Mystery dominates the film. It is at once a documentary on Paris, a gangster film, a spy film, and a horror film, a Greek tragedy, a Shakespeare play, a psychiatric study, a metaphysical meditation, an application of Einsteinian relativity, and an indictment of fascism. And so Rivette's world is both subject and object of one of the richest *Weltanschauung* that has ever been brought to the screen. As such, it concerns us all.' And, a week later, replying to letters: 'Let's get things straight: *Paris Nous Appartient* is a nonentity' (*France-Observateur*, No. 608, December 1961).

From the very start we feel at sea, and we feel this is what the director deliberately intended. Anne, whose attention is caught by a strange groaning sound, comes out of her tiny bedsitter and finds, in another little room on the same landing, a young woman sobbing, who assures her that 'the hour is nigh', that 'waiting is difficult', and speaks of Hiroshima as though the destruction of the world were to be found in Nostradamus or in that eternal guiding myth, the Bible. Anne charitably tries to console her: 'leave me alone,' says the woman, 'I can't go on. In any case, it doesn't matter, no one can do anything more for me.' And just to hammer the last nail in the coffin, she adds that 'no one will escape the common lot', and that 'the world is threatened'. And so we suppose that we poor shadows are well on the way to being totally removed from the face of the earth, because there exist ferocious and terrifying organisa-

Paris Nous Appartient: the young woman sobbing

tions which swoop down on people and destroy them. This at least
is what Philip Kaufman declares, but when Anne wants to know
more he answers back: 'I am certain of nothing.' So things get more
and more obscure: 'If it is necessary to retain obscurity in order
not to distort reality, let's keep it. Anyway, reality itself is often
obscure' (interview in *Clarté*, No. 41, February 1962). Especially
as 'the biggest fool is the person who thinks he has the truth. Philip
is half crazy, it's significant' (*ibid.*). This is probably the profound
reason why the walls of Philip's flat are covered with little objects
that look like monsters, skeletons, or shrunken heads: it allows the
human beings to be surrounded by a décor of Anguish, Suffering,
and Approaching Death, and convinces us that Philip is hysterical.
Paris Nous Appartient ends with Gérard's suicide and another of
Philip's crises: we are doubtless supposed to realise that we are still
at sea, that this absurd world does not easily yield the truth, which
should be looked for – why not? – among epileptics! As far as the
last shot is concerned, it is remarkable for its blurred listlessness:

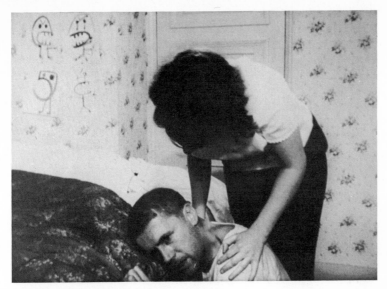

Paris Nous Appartient: Philip's flat

there are the gloomy waters of the Lac d'Ermenonville, gloomy birds, a gloomy sky, and faces as long as death; it is not at all difficult to recognise here the entire condition of contemporary man.

Before she got to know Gérard, Terry had a Spanish guitarist, Juan, as a lover. It seems he was very talented, and when he died he left some recorded guitar music somewhere or other. Gérard insists on trying to find this record in order to use it for his production of *Pericles*. Rivette's brainwave was to have made this record a symbol of the Truth that is being sought for all through the film: Anne tries to find Juan's will out of love for Gérard and his play. *Kiss Me Deadly* tried using the same device, but it is significant that here a work of art should replace the catastrophic Pandora's Box. It may be that the twentieth century is doomed to destruction, but people of quality, who, being sensitive and emotional, are secretly hostile to all kinds of forced political commitment, know just how exquisitely fragile Man is, and persist in protesting in his name. Poets, Beacons, Witnesses, Guides, Seers, Lights, Wise Men,

Paris Nous Appartient: the gloomy waters of the lake

Mountebanks, anyone you like, they all talk, in their Messages, of the imminence of the Apocalypse and of the oppression of slaves crushed beneath the weight of social order.

Fritz Lang (quoted in the film with an extract from *Metropolis*) is one of these. It is no coincidence that Rivette made Gérard an artist, and it is not merely an autobiographical need; Rivette, like Bazin, believes in Art as a total demystification of society. It would have been vulgar to have made Gérard a skilled worker or a hairdresser. In order to bear witness to the anguish of his age, he has to be a stage producer. The hero of *Le Signe du Lion* is an artist too: a composer and violinist. The pianist of *Tirez sur le Pianiste* is thrice smitten by Destiny, but he still has his piano. The *petits bourgeois* love to imagine that art is not a job but a vocation, a priesthood, and that the only hope left to man in this 'rotten' world is Creation in the form of completely purified Work. After Gérard's suicide, Jean-Val, his ex-assistant, takes over the rehearsals of *Pericles* without trying to find out where exactly the truth is to be found, and whether somebody was killed, and if so, by whom: 'The theatre,' said Gérard, 'is not an illusion but a reality.' Truffaut goes one better and says that 'the only thing left is the struggle to make the purity of the theatrical vocation triumph' (*Arts*, 6 August 1958). In the context of a politically apathetic civilisation that has been deformed by 'specialists', the artist will henceforth regard his work as an outlet, and by making himself a specialist too he will hoist himself out of the rut of everyday life. Presumably the main fault of a car factory worker is that he is not an artist, for if he were he would not adopt the cause of a party or a union or any system of any kind (except of capitalist exploitation of course), and as he would not be a union member he would not be bashed on the head by blacklegs in the pay of the employers.

The best sequences of the film are not the most ambitious ones. They are those that describe the life and work of actors in Paris. Perhaps they are acted a little listlessly at times, but they are admirably conceived and directed. The explanation is simple: these scenes are the only ones which give a little life to a particular concrete and topical problem – that of the actor in present-day France. Apart from them, *Paris Nous Appartient* is a *thin* film. The idea that underlies it is a hollow kernel: the characters, the images, the details, and the situations do not exist, and this should not surprise us. A film is a good film only when the situation depicted reveals the reasons which make it necessarily as it is. This presupposes a culture, an aim, experience, and organisation. Then and only then is there a chance that the spectator, too, will discover the amazing organisation of reality. That is why it can be said that the idea arises in the spectator from an organised spectacle and that the meaning of a film emerges from its temporal form instead of preceding it. Brecht's art, at least, is based on this idea.

But if someone comes along and says that *Paris Nous Appartient* portrays the uncertainty, the confusion, the 'equivocality' of our existence and our age, then I say 'Long live Bazin! But leave Brecht out of it.' I mean by this that Rivette is making a fool of us and of himself when he sees himself already evolving towards a Brechtian manner: 'I'd like to follow the example of Brecht: *Paris Nous*

Paris Nous Appartient: 'Where are we going?'

Appartient would be *Drums in the Night*; and the trilogy I am
planning set in the eighteenth century, more or less an adaptation
of *Edward II*' (*Clarté*, No. 41, February 1962). The Brechtian
spectacle defines the how and why of the situation it describes; it
is an effort to reveal the true organisation of society and expose its
contradictions. It requires a demonstration, a 'dismantling', to
make the spectator grasp this. Its purpose is radically different from
that of Rivette: Brecht is never ambiguous. That is why not only
conservatives but 'liberals' hate him.

On the contrary, in *Paris Nous Appartient*, Terry, as dawn
approaches, tells Philip to get into her car: 'Where are we going?'
asks Philip, who has not yet got over his crisis. 'Oh, we'll see,'
replies Terry. This is not methodical doubt, nor is it a decision to
ask real questions; it is the country priest's sermon, it is a wreath of
mist that is gingerly wafted across the scene. I feel that *Paris Nous
Appartient* is fairly representative of the Nouvelle Vague, and offers
rather an accurate definition of the present state of the *bourgeoisie*,

which, in order to get out of a class struggle which is anything but avoidable, has chosen scepticism as its motto: 'I shall probably never make socially or politically committed films, for in this field, the field of problems, it is no longer sufficient to leave question-marks. One has to contribute constructive ideas, assertions, perhaps even solutions. My doubts, my scepticism, my deep conviction that everyone has his reasons [Renoir again] would only add to the confusion.' 'Le Petit Soldat is political to the extent that the developments of the plot are due to political motives, but it can also be said that the film is not political because I don't take sides with anybody and because the subject is not orientated as it is in Russian films' (interview with J.-L. Godard in Le Monde, 13 September 1960). One can understand that some people are reluctant to class Paris Nous Appartient as a left- or right-wing film: it is clearly an 'anti-political' or, as Rivette puts it, an 'anti-thesis' film. Rivette sees in Terry's cold murder of Pierre the decisive proof that innocent people will always get themselves killed, by left-wing fanatics as well as by right-wing fanatics, for, at the same moment, we learn that Juan did not commit suicide but was liquidated by the Falangists. The Left and the Right have the same vices.

We should not allow ourselves to be hoodwinked into believing that Paris Nous Appartient really portrays some kind of revolt of Eternal Man against the Bureaucrats and Commissars of every country, or of Human Dignity against all kinds of fascism. All one can say is that the portrayal is dull and insipid. Paris Nous Appartient does not truly deal with the atomic peril or with people's general political attitudes or with the behaviour of our contemporaries; and Rivette is no new Plato, or if he is he can only serve us up with flimsy idées reçues. Can you really see the Truth in a fight between Negroes in a tunnel? Indeed, I don't believe any Nouvelle Vague film has tried harder to put up smoke-screens and brick walls for the spectators and actors to bash their heads against (walls, Kafka, Plato's cave, get it?), so that someone who has not understood a thing should come out of the cinema saying: it is the work of a genius, it's just what I felt without being able to express it.

We on Positif feel there is nothing for us to understand in a slipshod hotchpotch such as this, however subtle it may be, and that, using realism and 'up-to-dateness' as a pretext, the artist has no right to give us a chaotic portrayal of a chaotic period – he should try rather to fathom it; we are not ashamed to state and state again that *Paris Nous Appartient*, like *A Bout de Souffle*, lures fools into taking it seriously. At a time when various forces throughout the world are fighting each other and are winning or being defeated according to a pattern of history, Rivette has made one of the most 'obscurantist' films of the Nouvelle Vague. And so one can perhaps consider Rivette as a kind of Ionesco of the Champs-Élysées. The seductiveness of fascism has not affected him as it once did the author of *The Bald Primadonna* who has since changed his tune a bit, but the 'religious roots' (metaphysical, as they say) are always present. Under the pretext of defending Man, the idea is to attack the governing systems and committed individuals who create and uphold them: 'Those people,' says Terry, 'who want to destroy everything and who start by destroying themselves.' The main purpose is to safeguard eternal (or traditional, if you like) values by pretending to believe that they are perpetually present behind the appearances of the modern world. In this, the Nouvelle Vague has fulfilled its role. It has shuffled the cards, it has made carelessness a prime virtue, it has distorted the critical aspect of scepticism and jettisoned its valuable side. The Nouvelle Vague has not made carefreeness and humour liberating elements, but instead nice discreet digs at a Fate that could not care a damn, which is taken by them to be classical tragedy one day and romantic poetry the next.

Without realising how silly he is being, Chabrol replies to Sadoul's inquiry into 'Neo-romanticism in the Nouvelle Vague' as follows: 'Yes, I am a neo-romantic because we are living in a romantic period.' The hero of *A Bout de Souffle* protests against the inability of human beings to communicate with each other (what, again?) and tries to live out a frenzied individuality which proves to be less individual than the behaviour of Jean Seberg; he calls himself Laszlo Kowacs just to show that he is disowning his origins, just as the hero of *Le Signe du Lion* has no homeland: 'I am a bit of everything – Austrian, American, Swiss.' *Paris Nous Appartient* teems with

exiles and misfits: the man expelled from the USA is the brother of
the émigré from Budapest (who lives in the same hotel as he does)
and of the Spaniard we met in the drawing-room in Neuilly; and,
in the very first shots of the film, we see sweet Anne being bored to
death by her English lessons, which only goes to show that she too
is a misfit. A great primordial nobility, a marked thirst for purity,
an elevation of the feelings – all characterise these individuals: 'The
hero of *Le Petit Soldat* is right-wing, and at the same time he is left-
wing because he is sentimental' (*ibid.*). A character in *Le Signe du
Lion* says of the hero of the film: 'He is a weak but good man.' How
curious *Le Signe du Lion* is: Rohmer wanted to show the omni-
presence of Fate by following a violinist who wanders round Paris
and becomes a tramp because it never crosses Rohmer's mind to
make him earn a living. This is, of course, supposed to emphasise
'the essential loneliness' of Man.

For Rohmer, then, the walk along the banks of the Seine becomes
the woe of the lonely man who is hounded by the idiotic immanence
of civilisation and the indifference of nature: water, stone, crowds.
Compare Joris Ivens's Seine, in *La Seine a Rencontré Paris*, the
product of human labour, which canalises and orders nature. And
what would be the point of making Pierre, the hero of the film, work
anyway? For just at the moment when he sinks to the bottom of the
abyss, he is saved by an inheritance and made a rich man. The
camera confirms the miracle: it pans from the bottom of the church
of Saint-Germain-des-Près up to the top of its spire and into
Universal Night. 'I believe profoundly,' says François Truffaut
elsewhere, 'in original sin and in the metaphysical aspect of life.'

This is classicism if you like, but it is withered classicism. It is
romanticism if you like, but it is meagre romanticism. There is
however a tremendous ambition: to portray individual dramas and
set them against the background of collective dramas – to be the
Balzac of our time. The Balzac or the Resnais? The place has
already been filled, well and truly filled. *Hiroshima, Mon Amour* is
the perfect illustration of the dreams of the Nouvelle Vague; but
Resnais alone is capable of realising them because he never poses
the problem in the jumbled form of a 'film-discussion on life,

Hiroshima Mon Amour

liberty, death, and anguish'. (interview in *Clarté*, No. 41, February 1962). As far as Rivette is concerned, the definition needed is: *petit bourgeois* romanticism in the manner of Jean Sarment (and who reads Jean Sarment nowadays?) as opposed to the very different romanticism of the *bourgeois* Hugo or the *bourgeois* Barrès, as opposed to the masterly and virile fantasy of *Kiss Me Deadly* and the powerful conceptions of Alain Resnais. It is the *petit bourgeois* romanticism of a cry-baby who is afraid of both past and future. 'In the last thirty years,' says Philip Kaufman, 'methods have changed. . . . All those who refuse to yield to Efficiency, the Establishment, Technique, are simply crushed.' There can be no doubt that Philip is here speaking for the director. And yet methods of oppression have always existed and have always been brutal: the Romans crucified Spartacus, the Inquisition burnt heretics, the Yankees shot the Indians, colonialists burn down Negro villages, and policemen beat up strikers. Why the limitative 'In the last thirty years'? Probably for the same reasons Godard puts forward when he says he would be incapable of making a film about the Resistance: 'There was a way of talking and feeling that has no connection with our present-day behaviour (interview with J.-L. Godard in *Le Monde*, 13 September 1960). *Petits bourgeois* not only fear the future (and consequently do not even try to conceive of it) but they are also afraid of looking too closely at the History they have mastered. They would find there the image of their own shabbiness and the sources of a romanticism they believe to have originated – in fact their own is the sign of a total inability to come to grips effectively with a historical movement that is certainly bloody but none the less alive. André Bazin would, I think, have liked *Paris Nous Appartient*.

From a booklet devoted to the Nouvelle Vague by Raymond Borde, I quote the following portrait of the new type of hero given to us by the films of Vadim, which could also serve as the portrait of many Nouvelle Vague central characters: 'He says little, and puts on an air of controlled suffering. He is both a priest *manqué* and an aristocrat. He is the incarnation of the young introverted right-wing that has lost the picturesque quality that the royalists of *Action Française* had. He is supposed to hint at some kind of metaphysical torment; he looks elegantly pained; in short, he is striking an attitude. He is a misogynist. . . . He keeps his distance, dreams perhaps of the Old Régime and goes along with the new one. What strikes me most about him is the lack of any sign of being "anti" ' (*Premier Plan*, 10, p. 12). Philip Esnault is also to the point: 'The profound anaemia of the young film-makers can be explained by the situation of a generation that does not know what to do with itself and by the very real confusion of the *bourgeoise élite* from which they issue, by the intellectual and moral suffocation that is caused by a certain Parisian way of life. Nothing is more difficult to express than a mentality of refusal, a spirit of affectation, an attitude of escapism. Nothing is easier than to clutch on to myths and masters. Will our film-makers of tomorrow be anything more than mere disciples? Their social scepticism camouflages their great respect for money as a liberator, and their scepticism in sex camouflages a romantic belief in shared happiness. The theme of failure immediately shows through, since salvation through love is made impossible by other people. But it is clear that this loneliness is more metaphysical than social. We may have the nasty feeling that, when reference is made to the celebrated "interior realism" or when pure statement is used as a pretext, all that is being hidden is a shunning of responsibilities . . .' (*Les Lettres Françaises*, March-April 1960).

In this study, I have approached only a few of the questions raised by André Bazin. His system and its development remain to be studied in depth: its connections with the philosophy of Teilhard de Chardin, Lachelier, or the 'naïve beliefs' of Daniel Rops, and its practical application by critics of daily, weekly, or monthly journals. There are other aspects too which I have not had the time or the energy to approach. However the system can be summed up as follows: its starting-point is the ontology of the cinema, its essence, and for convenience's sake it brushes aside such aspects as History, Economics, Politics, Technique, Society, etc.

At the end of this inquiry, one is naturally prompted to ask a fundamental question: what happened to French criticism which, between 1945 and 1958, gave such confused and implicitly reactionary conceptions as those of Bazin the freedom of the city, and allowed them to become part of our daily lives? It is natural that right-wing critics should welcome a critical system that lies at the crossroads of so many traditions – *bourgeois*, idealist, liberal, religious, and social democrat. It is natural that right-wing critics should not scorn a 'dialectic' that cleverly combines the prestige of rationalism and the irrational powers of the image, borrowing the linguistic charms from the former, and the guiles of faith from the latter. It is natural that right-wing critics should agree with a system which rejects the notion of 'committedness' and gives pride of place to 'psychological' or 'moral' criteria. It is less natural that such left-wing critics as Sadoul and Albert Cervoni should consider Bazin to be respectively 'the best French critic' and 'a remarkable dialectician' (*Positif*, 36, 'Inquiry into left-wing criticism'). One's only answer can be that Marxist criticism in France has revealed its lack of seriousness, its lack of criteria, at the very time it most needed to be lucid.

It seems to me that Cervoni's summing-up of Bazin holds one of the keys to the problem: 'Bazin, a left-wing critic, was neither Marxist nor even materialist.' That, in black and white, means that the old Marxist and materialist notions must be revised, since a spiritual and non-Marxist system is here considered enough to make a 'left-wing critic'. Which means that without needing to analyse a situation portrayed in a film from a Marxist, or even materialist, standpoint, one can still end up with good concrete results, with a 'criticism' and a 'demystification' of *bourgeois* values and the *bourgeois* order. Or else, if left-wing criticism can be conceived of outside the sphere of a radical attack on the *bourgeois* system and ideology, one is supposed to accept the specious arguments of reformist criticism. 'I would say,' Cervoni goes on, 'that an entirely honest critic is pretty close to becoming a left-wing critic, if he has not already become one.' This is the stunt of the 'ray of sunlight', of the resolutely *optimistic* critic. There is clearly no longer any need to be a Marxist, let alone a materialist, in order to become a left-wing critic. You just need to be honest, to be quite simply a man, to exist. The notions of revolt, analysis, and effectiveness are lost in the darkness of time. And probably because the French public is on the whole less receptive today to a Marxist approach and method of analysis, Marxism is left, with its accomplice, materialism, in the cloakroom. This makes the public happy. But through wanting to reconcile opposites, the Left is losing ground every day without realising it. It is caught between two stools: on the one side, it is stubborn on a strictly political level (for instance, in the argument between *Humanité-Dimanche* and Bazin in February 1956 about censorship, the Church, and Catholic criticism; or else in the violent quarrel which pitted Sadoul against Bazin on the question of Bazin's brilliant and remarkable article on 'The myth of Stalin in the Soviet cinema' (*Esprit*, August 1950); and on the other side, the Left respects social-democrat ideology so as not to cut itself off from eventual allies; in fact, this ideology is sometimes even adopted, adapted, and imbibed. Should such tactics be considered a sign of 'increasing carelessness and unbridled eclecticism' (Roland Barthes), of 'complacent slavery' (Borde), of simple mimicry, or the result of supremely adroit conduct? One

Les Yeux sans Visage

cannot answer at the moment except by looking at the evidence as it comes in. The results are not very brilliant. Marcel Martin is well aware of this, when he regrets that no one denounced, if not 'André Bazin man of the Left", at least 'his uprooted aestheticism which is an indisputable feature of right-wing criticism' (*Positif*, 36, 'Inquiry into left-wing criticism').

In fact, a lot of damage has been done. It is easy to poke fun at the hazy distinguishing marks of Bazin's system, but there can be no doubt that Bazin, although he did not create his disciples (they would have existed without him), helped to cement fallacious theories and give them that appearance of solidity which permits even the most insubstantial of ideas to keep out of danger. Bazin was somebody who united what should have been disrupted. His heir today is Georges Sadoul. Sadoul, too, tries to put everything on the same level, instead of looking for contradictions and creating oppositions. Not only does he attempt to link the new French cinema with the generations that have preceded it (for example,

Jacques Demy's *Lola* with the tradition of 'poetic realism') but he also puts widely differing directors into the same basket by talking of a 'Paris school', a '1960 generation', a 'neo-romanticism', and the list, alas, has not been completed. On the contrary, some films should have been criticised and others defended, in order to encourage what was good in the French cinema. A new cinema which has been able within the last few years, to offer us such films as *Hiroshima, Mon Amour*, *L'Année Dernière à Marienbad*, *Une Vie*, *Moi Un Noir*, *Zazie dans le Métro*, *Cuba Si!*, *L'Enclos*, *Les Yeux Sans Visage*, *Marines* (to quote only a few films without going back too far) does not need to be defended *en bloc*; but it does demand that the grain be separated very carefully from the chaff. Is there a new French cinema? Yes, as long as two mistakes are avoided: opposing it to the old, *en bloc*, and linking it with the old, *en bloc*.

There can be no doubt that André Bazin was a man of taste and a scrupulous critic. None of his articles is botched, and that in itself is a recommendation. Sometimes even, when he managed to tear himself away from his beloved ambiguities and went into the attack, he could produce good strong stuff: articles such as 'The myth of Stalin in the Soviet cinema' and 'La Politique des Auteurs' are more than ever relevant. This good side of Bazin remains to be studied. But Bazin did have to be put in his proper place, and not left in a false situation that was a little too reminiscent of de Gaulle at the helm of the Ship of State, or of Pope John XXIII blessing Italian Christians and socialists just before his 'opening towards the Left': 'They are all my little children.'

Gozlan mentions Bazin's article on the politique des auteurs *as one of the few he likes. It is also remarkable for showing the gap, narrow on the surface but in fact quite wide, between the critical positions of Bazin and his disciples.*

The term politique des auteurs (*literally 'the policy of authors'*) *is* a vague one, and has been used to encompass a number of widely differing attitudes. *Understood in the sense of a faithfulness to certain directors and a willingness to champion them through the thick and thin of their inspiration, it is a term which applies more accurately to the critics of* Positif *than of* Cahiers. Positif's *favourite directors (*Buñuel, Welles, Ford, Huston, Minnelli, Fellini, Antonioni, *to mention but a few) have remained more or less constant. But* Cahiers *has a long record of fickle tastes: first there were the grotesquely styled 'hitchcockohawksiens', then the worshippers of Lang, Losey, Sirk, and Walsh, then the fanatics who swore by Edgar G. Ulmer and Riccardo Freda, and so on. Bazin's own tastes, however, always remained constant, personal, and, in both senses of the word, catholic.*

The term politique des auteurs *also took on a new shade of meaning. As the cinema in general, but especially the American cinema, tends to be an industry in which the personality of the director can easily be swamped, those directors came to be admired who managed somehow to get their personality across in spite of pressures against it such as an imposed script, imposed sets, imposed stars, etc. As the next step, the quality of a film was sometimes measured solely in terms of the amount of individual personality the director had been clever enough to slip into it, irrespective of whether that personality were interesting in the first place, irrespective of his preoccupations and themes, if any.*

Needless to say, Bazin had his feet too firmly on the ground to subscribe to this kind of inane attitude to films. In his article on the politique des auteurs, *he mounts a convincing attack on the distorters of this theory and, incidentally, on those who are prone, as is* Positif *occasionally, to suppose that a good director can never make a bad film.*

9: La politique des auteurs

André Bazin

'Goethe? Shakespeare? Everything they put their name to is supposed to be good, and people rack their brains to find beauty in the silliest little. thing they bungled. All great talents, like Goethe, Shakespeare, Beethoven, Michelangelo, created not only beautiful works, but things that were less than mediocre, quite simply awful.' Tolstoy, *Diary 1895–99.*

I realise my task is fraught with difficulties. *Cahiers du Cinéma* is thought to practise the *politique des auteurs.* This opinion may perhaps not be justified by the entire output of articles, but it has been true of the majority, especially for the last two years. It would be useless and hypocritical to point to a few scraps of evidence to the contrary, and claim that our magazine is a harmless collection of wishywashy reviews.

Nevertheless, our readers must have noticed that this critical standpoint – whether implicit or explicit – has not been adopted with equal enthusiasm by all the regular contributors to *Cahiers*, and that there might exist serious differences in our admiration, or rather in the degree of our admiration. And yet the truth is that the most enthusiastic among us nearly always win the day. Eric Rohmer put his finger on the reason in his reply to a reader in No. 64: 'When opinions differ on an important film, we generally prefer to let the person who likes it most write about it'. It follows that the strictest adherents of the *politique des auteurs* get the best of it in the end, for, rightly or wrongly, they always see in their favourite directors the manifestation of the same specific qualities. So it is that Hitchcock,

Renoir, Rossellini, Lang, Hawks, or Nicholas Ray, to judge from the pages of *Cahiers*, appear as almost infallible directors who could never make a bad film.

I would like to avoid a misunderstanding from the start. I beg to differ with those of my colleagues who are the most firmly convinced that the *politique des auteurs* is well founded, but this in no way compromises the general policy of the magazine. Whatever our differences of opinion about films or directors, our common likes and dislikes are numerous enough and strong enough to bind us together; and although I do not see the role of the *auteur* in the cinema in the same way as François Truffaut or Eric Rohmer for example, it does not stop me believing to a certain extent in the concept of the *auteur* and very often sharing their opinions, although not always their passionate loves. I fall in with them more reluctantly in the case of their hostile reactions; often they are very harsh with films I find defensible – and I do so precisely because I find that the work transcends the director (they dispute this phenomenon, which they consider to be a critical contradiction). In other words, almost our only difference concerns the relationship between the work and its creator. I have never been sorry that one of my colleagues has stuck up for such and such director, although I have not always agreed about the qualities of the film under examination. Finally, I would like to add that although it seems to me that the *politique des auteurs* has led its supporters to make a number of mistakes, its total results have been fertile enough to justify them in the face of their critics. It is very rare that the arguments drawn upon to attack them do not make me rush to their defence.

So it is within these limits, which, if you like, are those of a family quarrel, that I would like to tackle what seems to me to represent not so much a critical mistranslation as a critical 'false nuance of meaning'. My point of departure is an article by my friend Jean Domarchi on Vincente Minnelli's *Lust for Life*, which tells the story of Van Gogh. His praise was very intelligent and sober, but it struck me that such an article should not have been published in a review which, only one month previously, had allowed Eric Rohmer to demolish John Huston. The relentless harshness of the latter, and the indulgent admiration of the former, can only be explained by the fact that Minnelli is one of Domarchi's favourites and that Huston is not a *Cahiers auteur*. This partiality is a good thing, up to a certain point, as it leads us to stick up for a film that illustrates certain facets of American culture just as much as the personal talent of Vincente Minnelli. I could get Domarchi caught up in a contradiction, by pointing out to him that he ought to have sacrificed Minnelli in favour of Renoir, since it was the shooting of *Lust for Life* that forced the director of *French Cancan* to give up his own project on Van Gogh. Can Domarchi claim that a *Van Gogh* by Renoir would not have brought more prestige to the *politique des auteurs* than a film by Minnelli? What was needed was a painter's son, and what we got was a director of filmed ballets!

But whatever the case, this example is only a pretext. Many a time I have felt uneasy at the subtlety of an argument, which was completely unable to camouflage the *naïveté* of the assumption whereby, for example, the intentions and the coherence of a deliberate and well thought out film are read into some little 'B' feature.

And of course as soon as you state that the film-maker and his films are one, there can be no minor films, as the worst of them will always be in the image of their creator. But let's see what the facts of the matter are. In order to do so, we must go right back to the beginning.

Of course, the *politique des auteurs* is the application to the cinema of a notion that is widely accepted in the individual arts. François Truffaut likes to quote Giraudoux's remark: 'There are no works, there are only *auteurs*' – a polemical sally which seems to me of limited significance. The opposite statement could just as well be set as an exam question. The two formulae, like the maxims of La Rochefoucauld and Chamfort, would simply reverse their proportion of truth and error. As for Eric Rohmer, he states (or rather asserts) that in art it is the *auteurs*, and not the works, that remain; and the programmes of film societies would seem to support this critical truth.

But one should note that Rohmer's argument does not go nearly as far as Giraudoux's aphorism, for, if *auteurs* remain, it is not necessarily because of their production as a whole. There is no lack of examples to prove that the contrary is true. Maybe Voltaire's name is more important than his bibliography, but now that he has been put in perspective it is not so much his *Dictionnaire Philosophique* that counts nowadays as his Voltairean wit, a certain *style* of thinking and writing. But today where are we to find the principle and the example ? In his abundant and atrocious writings for the theatre ? Or in the slim volume of short stories ? And what about Beaumarchais ? Are we to go looking in *La Mère Coupable* ?

In any case, the authors of that period were apparently themselves aware of the relativity of their worth, since they willingly disowned their works, and sometimes even did not mind being the subject of lampoons whose quality they took as a compliment. For them, almost the only thing that mattered was the work itself, whether their own or another's, and it was only at the end of the eighteenth century, with Beaumarchais in fact, that the concept of the *auteur* finally crystallised legally, with his royalties, duties, and responsibilities. Of course I am making allowances for historical and social contingencies; political and moral censorship has made anonymity sometimes inevitable and always excusable. But surely the anonymity of the writings of the French Resistance in no way lessened the dignity or responsibility of the writer. It was only in the nineteenth century that copying or plagiarism really began to be considered a professional breach that disqualified its perpetrator.

The same is true of painting. Although nowadays any old splash of paint can be valued according to its measurements and the celebrity of the signature, the objective quality of the work itself was formerly held in much higher esteem. Proof of this is to be found in the difficulty there is in authenticating a lot of old pictures. What emerged from a studio might simply be the work of a pupil, and we are now unable to *prove* anything one way or the other. If one goes back even further, one has to take into consideration the anonymous works that have come down to us as the products not of an artist, but of an art, not of a man, but of a society.

I can see how I will be rebutted. We should not objectify our ignorance or let it crystallise into a reality. All these works of art,

140

the Venus de Milo as well as the Negro mask, did in fact have an *auteur*; and the whole of modern historical science is tending to fill in the gaps and give names to these works of art. But did one really have to wait for such erudite addenda before being able to admire and enjoy them? Biographical criticism is but one of many possible critical dimensions – people are still arguing about the identity of Shakespeare or Molière.

But that's just the point! People *are* arguing. So their identity is not a matter of complete indifference. The evolution of Western art towards greater personalisation should definitely be considered as a step forward, as a refinement of culture, but only as long as this individualisation remains only a final perfection and does not claim to *define* culture. At this point, we should remember that irrefutable commonplace we learnt at school: the individual transcends society, but society is also and above all *within* him. So there can be no definitive criticism of genius or talent which does not first take into consideration the social determinism, the historical combination of circumstances, and the technical background which to a large extent determine it. That is why the anonymity of a work of art is a handicap that impinges only very slightly on our understanding of it. In any case, much depends on the particular branch of art in question, the style adopted, and the sociological context. Negro art does not suffer by remaining anonymous – although of course it is unfortunate we know so little about the societies that gave birth to it.

But *The Man Who Knew Too Much*, *Europe 51*, and *Bigger Than Life* are contemporary with the paintings of Picasso, Matisse, and Singier! Does it follow that one should see in them the same degree of individualisation? I for one do not think so.

If you will excuse yet another commonplace, the cinema is an art which is both popular and industrial. These conditions, which are necessary to its existence, in no way constitute a collection of hindrances – no more than in architecture – they rather represent a group of positive and negative circumstances which have to be reckoned with. And this is especially true of the American cinema, which the theoreticians of the *politique des auteurs* admire so much. What makes Hollywood so much better than anything else in the

Bigger than Life

world is not only the quality of certain directors, but also the vitality
and, in a certain sense, the excellence of a tradition. Hollywood's
superiority is only incidentally technical; it lies much more in what
one might call the American cinematic genius, something which
should be analysed, then defined, by a sociological approach to its
production. The American cinema has been able, in an extraordinarily competent way, to show American society just as it
wanted to see itself; but not at all passively, as a simple act of
satisfaction and escape, but dynamically, i.e. by participating with

the means at its disposal in the building of this society. What is so admirable in the American cinema is that it cannot help being spontaneous. Although the fruit of free enterprise and capitalism – and harbouring their active or still only virtual defects – it is in a way the truest and most realistic cinema of all because it shrinks from depicting even the contradictions of that society.

But it follows that every director is swept along by this powerful surge; naturally his artistic course has to be plotted according to the currents – it is not as if he were sailing as his fancy took him on the calm waters of a lake.

In fact it is not even true of the most individual artistic disciplines that genius is free and always self-dependent. And what is genius anyway if not a certain combination of unquestionably personal talents, a gift from the fairies, and a moment in history? Genius is an H-bomb. The fission of uranium triggers off the fusion of hydrogen pulp. But a sun cannot be born from the disintegration of an individual alone unless this disintegration has repercussions on the art that surrounds it. Whence the paradox of Rimbaud's life. His poetic flash in the pan suddenly died out and Rimbaud the adventurer became more and more distant like a star, still glowing but heading towards extinction. Probably Rimbaud did not change at all. There was simply nothing left to feed the flames that had reduced the whole of literature to ashes. Generally, the rhythm of this combustion in the cycles of great art is usually greater than the lifespan of a man. Literature's step is measured in centuries. It will be said that genius foreshadows that which comes after it. This is true, but only dialectically. For one could also say that every age has the geniuses it needs in order to define, repudiate, and transcend itself. Consequently, Voltaire was a horrible playwright when he thought he was Racine's successor and a story-teller of genius when he made the parable a vehicle for the ideas which were going to shatter the eighteenth century.

And even without having to use as examples the utter failures which had their causes almost entirely in the sociology of art, creative psychology alone could easily account for a lot of patchiness even in the best authors. *Notre-Dame-de-Paris* is pretty slight compared with *La Légende des Siècles, Salammbô* does not come up to *Madame Bovary,* or *Corydon* to *Le Journal des Faux-Monnayeurs.* There is no point in quibbling about these examples, there will always be others to suit everyone's taste. Surely one can accept the permanence of talent without confusing it with some kind of artistic infallibility or immunity against making mistakes, which could only be divine attributes. But God, as Sartre has already pointed out, is not an artist! Were one to attribute to creative man, in the face of all psychological probability, an unflagging richness of inspiration, one would have to admit that this inspiration always comes up against a whole complex of particular circumstances which make the result, in the cinema, a thousand times more chancy than in painting or in literature.

Inversely, there is no reason why there should not exist – and sometimes there do – flashes in the pan in the work of otherwise mediocre film-makers. Results of a fortunate combination of circumstances in which there is a precarious moment of balance between talent and milieu, these fleeting brilliancies do not prove all that much about personal creative qualities; but they are not however intrinsically inferior to others – and probably would not seem so if the critics had not begun by reading the signature at the bottom of the painting.

Well, what is true of literature is even truer of the cinema, to the extent that this art, the last to come on to the scene, accelerates and multiplies the evolutionary factors that are common to all the others. In fifty years, the cinema, which started with the crudest forms of spectacle (primitive but not inferior) has had to cover the same ground as the play or the novel and is often on the same level as they are. Within this same period, its technical development has been of a kind that cannot compare with that of any traditional art within a comparable period (except perhaps architecture, another industrial art). Under such conditions, it is hardly surprising that the genius will burn himself out ten times as fast, and that a director who suffers no loss of ability may cease to be swept along by the wave. This was the case with Stroheim, Abel Gance, and Orson Welles. We are now beginning to see things in enough perspective to notice a curious phenomenon: a film-maker can, within his own lifetime, be refloated by the following wave. This is true of Abel Gance or Stroheim, whose modernity is all the more apparent nowadays. I am fully aware that this only goes to prove their quality of *auteur*, but their eclipse still cannot be entirely explained away by the contradictions of capitalism or the stupidity of producers. If one keeps a sense of proportion, one sees that the same thing has happened to men of genius in the cinema as would have happened to a 120-year-old Racine writing Racinian plays in the middle of the eighteenth century. Would his tragedies have been better than Voltaire's? The answer is by no means clear-cut; but I bet they would not have been.

One can justifiably point to Chaplin, Renoir, or Clair. But each of them was endowed with further gifts that have little to do with genius and which were precisely those that enabled them to adapt themselves to the predicament of film production. Of course, the case of Chaplin was unique, since, as both *auteur* and producer, he has been able to be both the cinema and its evolution.

It follows then, according to the most basic laws of the psychology of creation, that, as the objective factors of genius are much more likely to modify themselves in the cinema than in any other art, a rapid maladjustment between the film-maker and the cinema can occur, and this can abruptly affect the quality of his films as a result. Of course I admire *Confidential Report*, and I can see the same qualities in it as I see in *Citizen Kane*. But *Citizen Kane* opened up a new era of American cinema, and *Confidential Report* is a film of only secondary importance.

But let's pause a moment on this assertion – it may, I feel, allow us to get to the heart of the matter. I think that not only would the supporters of the *politique des auteurs* refuse to agree that *Confidential Report* is an inferior film to *Citizen Kane*; they would be more eager to claim the contrary, and I can well see how they would go about it. As *Confidential Report* is Welles's sixth film, one can assume that a certain amount of progress has already been made. Not only did the Welles of 1953 have more experience of himself and of his art than in 1941, but however great was the freedom he was able to obtain in Hollywood *Citizen Kane* cannot help remaining to a

146

Confidential Report

certain extent an RKO product. The film would never have seen the light of day without the co-operation of some superb technicians and their just as admirable technical apparatus. Gregg Toland, to mention only one, was more than a little responsible for the final result. On the other hand, *Confidential Report* is completely the work of Welles. Until it can be proved to the contrary, it will be considered *a priori* a superior film because it is more personal and because Welles's personality can only have matured as he grew older.

As far as this question is concerned, I can only agree with my young firebrands when they state that age as such cannot diminish the talent of a film-maker and react violently to that critical prejudice which consists of always finding the works of a young or mature film-maker superior to the films of an old man. It has been said that *Monsieur Verdoux* was not up to *The Gold Rush*; people have criticised *The River* and *Carrosse d'Or*, saying they miss the good old days of *La Règle du Jeu*. Eric Rohmer has found an excellent answer to this: 'The history of art offers no example, as far as I know, of an authentic genius who has gone through a period of true decline at the end of his career; this should encourage us rather to detect, beneath what seems to be clumsy or bald, the traces of that desire for simplicity that characterises the "last manner" of painters such as Titian, Rembrandt, Matisse, or Bonnard, composers such as Beethoven and Stravinsky . . .' (*Cahiers*, 8, 'Renoir Américain'). What kind of absurd discrimination has decided that film-makers alone are victims of a senility that other artists are protected from? There do remain the exceptional cases of dotage, but they are much rarer than is sometimes supposed. When Baudelaire was paralysed and unable to utter anything other than his 'cré nom', was he any less Baudelairean? Robert Mallet tells us how Valéry Larbaud, Joyce's translator into French, struggling against paralysis after twenty years of immobility and silence, had managed to build up for himself a vocabulary of twenty simple words. With these, he was still able to bring out some extraordinarily shrewd literary judgements. In fact, the few exceptions one could mention only go to prove the rule. A great talent matures but does not grow old. There is no reason why this law of artistic psychology should not also be valid for the cinema. Criticism that is based implicitly on the hypothesis of senility cannot hold water. It is rather the opposite postulate that ought to be stated: we should say that when we think we can discern a decline it is our own critical sense that is at fault, since an impoverishment of inspiration is a very unlikely phenomenon. From this point of view, the bias of the *politique des auteurs* is very fruitful, and I will stick up for them against the *naïveté*, the foolishness even, of the prejudices they are fighting.

But, always remembering this, one has nevertheless to accept that certain indisputable 'greats' have suffered an eclipse or a loss of their powers. I think what I have already said in this article may point to the reason for this. The drama does not reside in the growing old of men but of the cinema: those who do not know how to grow old *with* it will be overtaken by its evolution. This is why it has been possible for there to have been a series of failures leading to complete catastrophe without it being necessary to suppose that the genius of yesterday has become an imbecile. Once again, it is simply a question of the appearance of a clash between the subjective inspiration of the creator and the objective situation of the cinema, and this is what the *politique des auteurs* refuses to see. To its supporters *Confidential Report* is a more important film than *Citizen Kane* because they justifiably see more of Orson Welles in it. In other words, all they want to retain in the equation *auteur plus subject = work* is the *auteur*, while the subject is reduced to zero. Some of them will pretend to grant me that, all things being equal as far as the *auteur* is concerned, a good subject is naturally better than a bad one, but the more outspoken and foolhardy among them will admit that it very much looks as if they prefer small 'B' films, where the banality of the scenario leaves more room for the personal contribution of the author.

Of course I will be challenged on the very concept of *auteur*. I admit that the equation I just used was artificial, just as much so in fact as the distinction one learnt at school between form and content. To benefit from the *politique des auteurs* one first has to be worthy of it, and as it happens this school of criticism claims to distinguish between true *auteurs* and directors, even talented ones: Nicholas Ray is an *auteur*, Huston is supposed to be only a director; Bresson and Rossellini are *auteurs*, Clément is only a great director, and so on. So this conception of the author is not compatible with the *auteur*/subject distinction, because it is of greater importance to find out if a director is worthy of entering the select group of *auteurs* than it is to judge how well he has used his material. To a certain extent at least, the *auteur* is a subject to himself; whatever the scenario, he always tells the same story, or, in case the word 'story' is confusing, let's say he has the same attitude and passes the same moral judgements on the action and on the characters. Jacques Rivette has said that an *auteur* is someone who speaks in the first person. It's a good definition; let's adopt it.

The *politique des auteurs* consists, in short, of choosing the personal factor in artistic creation as a standard of reference, and then of assuming that it continues and even progresses from one film to the next. It is recognised that there do exist certain important films of quality that escape this test, but these will systematically be considered inferior to those in which the personal stamp of the *auteur*, however run-of-the-mill the scenario, can be perceived even minutely.

It is far from my intention to deny the positive attitude and methodological qualities of this bias. First of all, it has the great merit of treating the cinema as an adult art and of reacting against the impressionistic relativism that still reigns over the majority of film reviews. I admit that the explicit or admitted pretension of a critic to reconsider the production of a film-maker with every new film in the light of his judgement has something presumptuous about it that recalls Ubu. I am also quite willing to admit that if one is human one cannot help doing this, and, short of giving up the whole idea of actually criticising, one might as well take as a starting-point the feelings, pleasant or unpleasant, one feels personally when in contact with a film. Okay, but only on condition that these first impressions are kept in their proper place. We have to take them into consideration, but we should not use them as a basis. In other words, every critical act should consist of referring the film in question to a scale of values, but this reference is not merely a matter of intelligence; the sureness of one's judgement arises also, or perhaps even first of all (in the chronological sense of the word), from a general impression experienced during a film. I feel there are two symmetrical heresies, which are (*a*) objectively applying to a film a critical all-purpose yardstick, and (*b*) considering it sufficient simply to state one's pleasure or disgust. The first denies the role of taste, the second presupposes the superiority of the critic's taste over that of the author. Coldness . . . or presumption!

What I like about the *politique des auteurs* is that it reacts against the impressionist approach while retaining the best of it. In fact the scale of values it proposes is not ideological. Its starting-point is an appreciation largely composed of taste and sensibility: it has to discern the contribution of the artist as such, quite apart from the qualities of the subject or the technique: i.e. the man behind the style. But once one has made this distinction, this kind of criticism is doomed to beg the question, for it assumes at the start of its analysis that the film is automatically good as it has been made by an *auteur*. And so the yardstick applied to the film is the aesthetic portrait of the film-maker deduced from his previous films. This is all right so long as there has been no mistake about promoting this film-maker to the status of *auteur*. For it is objectively speaking safer to trust in the genius of the artist than in one's own critical intelligence. And this is where the *politique des auteurs* falls in line with the system of 'criticism by beauty'; in other words, when one is dealing with a genius, it is always a good method to presuppose that a supposed weakness in a work of art is nothing other than a beauty that one has not yet managed to understand. But as I have shown this method had its limitations even in traditionally individualistic arts such as literature, and all the more so in the cinema where the sociological and historical cross-currents are countless. By giving such importance to 'B' films, the *politique des auteurs* recognises and confirms this dependence *a contrario*.

Another point is that as the criteria of the *politique des auteurs* are very difficult to formulate the whole thing becomes highly hazardous. It is significant that our finest writers on *Cahiers* have been practising it for three or four years now and have yet to produce the main corpus of its theory. Nor is one particularly likely to forget how Rivette suggested we should admire Hawks: 'The mark of Hawks's genius is evidence of fact; *Monkey Business* is the work of a genius, and it impresses itself on one's mind through this evidence. Some people resist against this, they demand more than simple affirmations. And perhaps the failure to appreciate his talent arises quite simply from this. . . .' You can see the danger: an aesthetic personality cult.

Monkey Business

But that is not the main point, at least to the extent that the *politique des auteurs* is practised by people of taste who know how to watch their step. It is its negative side that seems the most serious to me. It is unfortunate to praise a film that in no way deserves it, but the dangers are less far-reaching than when a worthwhile film is rejected because its director has made nothing good up to that point. I am not denying that the champions of the *politique des auteurs* discover or encourage a budding talent when they get the chance. But they do systematically look down on anything in a film that comes from a common fund and which can sometimes be entirely admirable, just as it can be utterly detestable. Thus, a certain kind of popular American culture lies at the basis of Minnelli's *Lust for Life*, but another more spontaneous kind of culture is also the principle of American comedy, the Western, and the gangster film. And its influence is here beneficial, for it is this that gives these cinematic genres their vigour and richness, resulting as they do from an artistic evolution that has always been in wonderfully close harmony with its public. And so one can read a review in *Cahiers* of a Western by Anthony Mann (and God knows I like Anthony Mann's Westerns!) as if it were not above all a Western, i.e. a whole collection of conventions in the script, the acting, and the direction. I know very well that in a film magazine one may be permitted to skip such mundane details; but they should at least be implied, whereas what in fact happens is that their existence is glossed over rather sheepishly, as though they were a rather ridiculous necessity that it would be incongruous to mention. In any case, they will look down on, or treat condescendingly, any Western by a director who is not yet approved, even if it is as round and smooth as an egg. Well, what is *Stagecoach* if not an ultra-classical Western in which the art of Ford consists simply of raising characters and situations to an absolute degree of perfection; and while sitting on the Censorship Committee I have seen some admirable Westerns, more or less anonymous and off the beaten track, but displaying a wonderful knowledge of the conventions of the genre and respecting the style from beginning to end.

Paradoxically, the supporters of the *politique des auteurs* admire the American cinema, where the restrictions of production are heavier than anywhere else. It is also true that it is the country where the greatest technical possibilities are offered to the director. But the one does not cancel out the other. I do however admit that freedom is greater in Hollywood than it is said to be, as long as one knows how to detect its manifestations, and I will go so far as to say that the tradition of genres is a base of operations for creative freedom. The American cinema is a classical art, but why not then admire in it what is most admirable, i.e. not only the talent of this or that filmmaker, but the genius of the system, the richness of its ever-vigorous tradition, and its fertility when it comes into contact with new elements – as has been proved, if proof there need be, in such films as *An American In Paris*, *The Seven Year Itch*, and *Bus Stop*. True, Logan is lucky enough to be considered an *auteur*, or at least a budding *auteur*. But then when *Picnic* or *Bus Stop* get good reviews the praise does not go to what seems to me to be the essential point, i.e. the social truth, which of course is not offered as a goal that suffices in itself but is integrated into a style of cinematic narration just as pre-war America was integrated into American comedy.

To conclude: the *politique des auteurs* seems to me to hold and defend an essential critical truth that the cinema needs more than the other arts, precisely because an act of true artistic creation is more uncertain and vulnerable in the cinema than elsewhere. But its exclusive practice leads to another danger: the negation of the film to the benefit of praise of its *auteur*. I have tried to show why mediocre *auteurs* can, by accident, make admirable films, and how, conversely, a genius can fall victim to an equally accidental sterility. I feel that this useful and fruitful approach, quite apart from its polemical value, should be complemented by other approaches to the cinematic phenomenon which will restore to a film its quality as a work of art. This does not mean one has to deny the role of the *auteur*, but simply give him back the preposition without which the noun *auteur* remains but a halting concept. *Auteur*, yes, but what *of* ?

Finally, I have included an article on the Nouvelle Vague in general by Robert Benayoun which is in its own way almost a manifesto. Positif was put in a difficult position at the time of the Nouvelle Vague. Its violent attack on the films of the Cahiers directors was interpreted by some, not least by Cahiers, as sour grapes. This was unfair in the light of the evidence. It was hardly likely that Positif would adore the films of those whose criticism they had been reacting against only a year previously. What they objected to was the fact that Cahiers gave the impression that they alone were the Nouvelle Vague. What about Resnais, Franju, Astruc, Malle, Demy, De Broca, Rozier, and the rest of them ? said Positif. Benayoun's article, aggressive and virulent though it is, is not merely destructive; it is a call for the kind of cinema that Positif believes in.

10: The king is naked

Robert Benayoun

'To measure a circle, one can begin anywhere.' Charles Fort.
'If the cinema looks in upon itself too much, it will be in danger of ending up as a kind of subculture, consisting of approximations, pale reflections, quotations, and hazy reminiscences; it will be as though it were shut up in a furnished flat whose walls were covered with photographs of furniture, whose books were only about furnishing.' Robert Benayoun: 'Against the Cinema of Furnishing.'

Have you been abroad recently?

There are two things which make foreign countries jealous of us: De Gaulle and the Nouvelle Vague.

And I'm not saying that just to be clever: observations from afar tend to synthesise, and the two subjects I have mentioned are not as unconnected as one might think at first glance.

French propaganda abroad uses the Nouvelle Vague (just as it does the liner *France*, or the oil-wells of Hassi-Messaoud) in order to prove that France is not, as has been suggested, a country of old men. It is only natural that use should be made, for this purpose, of such very young old men as the leaders of the Nouvelle Vague, who, like the government itself, are haunted by the touching desire to make a career and to *last*.*

---

*France can boast nothing less youthful than the group of film-makers who have emerged from *Cahiers du Cinéma*. They possess none of the normal qualities of youth: *naiveté*, idealism, humour, hatred of tradition, erotomania, a sense of injustice. Truffaut is as old as Cloche or Moguy, Chabrol as old as Duvivier, Godard as old as Malaparte. Only Jacques Rozier, an outsider, seems to be the same age as his heroes.

The Gaullist régime, like the Nouvelle Vague, still keeps up the illusion abroad with an unruffled display of contradictions, combined with shilly-shallying, hollow catchphrases, patriotic jingles, and a breezy use of clichés. It is characterised, as is the Nouvelle Vague, by an avowed determination to maintain confusion in order to stand its ground, by an unholy fear of intervention or rivalry from outside, and by a manifest propensity to amalgamate contradictory theses. Finally, De Gaulle (like the Nouvelle Vague) is trying to keep permanently at bay that moment when it will be apparent, as in the Andersen fairy-tale, that the king is naked.

Plenty of other comparisons will come to mind during the course of this article: it is quite clear that Gaullist France, with its raucous demagogy and its blindness to realities, was ideal ground for a school of ultra-*bourgeois* expression, based on diversion, compromise, and other feeble characteristics inherited from their elders.

I will be taken to task at once for the tone of this article. Why did I not opt for the stiff objectivity of the historian and cast over a movement that is five years old the veil that is usually destined for the millennia that sandwich Christ ? I must admit that I would have been incapable of doing so. To the young people of the Nickelodéon and Cinéquanon film societies, the year 1957 must have an aura of antediluvian legend, reminding them of the time when, with their voices hardly broken, they were refused entry to horror films; but in the bound volumes of the important trade paper, *La Cinématographie Française*, the Nouvelle Vague does not take up very much room. The films were more often phantasmal than palpable.

And so I'm going to be unfair. I may even go a bit too far and make a summary judgement of a film which might deserve a longer analysis. But the pamphleteer has the privilege of being able to lacerate something he does not completely abhor simply in order to clear the ground; he can point out the most obvious faults, and leave the filmologists to pick their way through the haystack. The lenience of film-lovers is notorious: put them in their leather seat in a darkened cinema and they will set off in search of that famous

Les Cousins

quarter of an hour which can redeem the most incompetent, but alluringly titled, film. And I'm not going to go into detailed discussion of the shots or sequences which, in such and such a Nouvelle Vague film, soothed my regrets at wasting time.

Let's make our point bluntly: the catchphrase 'Nouvelle Vague', which arose as everyone knows from an inquiry into youth by Françoise Giroud which appeared in *L'Express*, was first applied by that same weekly to a film by Marcel Carné called *Les Tricheurs*. The film was extraordinarily vulgar, redolent of the immediately post-war period. It was nevertheless well received, and the catchphrase made a hit. It was used again for *Les Cousins* and was, as we know, successful. And I would not fall into the bad habit of certain columnists who denigrate a film on the strength of its publicity handout, had not those responsible for *Cahiers du Cinéma*, whose pontifications hover glibly among the departed spirits of Heidegger, Malraux, and Korzybsky, themselves taken such enormous delight in the most unpleasant demands of this activity.

From 1958 onwards, a new kind of production was the done thing: a low budget, no stars, a small camera crew, a sensational subject, and some explosive publicity. The national Press was most co-operative. The members of the Nouvelle Vague had no difficulty in finding a mouthpiece, and they began to rewrite history. To quote Godard, that master-purveyor of hot air: 'I purposely shot the film at great speed, it was an improvised rough job. . . . People had never shot a film like that before.' And elsewhere: 'Studio sets are never constructed with a ceiling to them. . . . The walls were painted white, something that's never done in film-making.' French newsreels were astonished that any-one dared, *for the first time*, to camouflage a camera in the middle of a street in order to film passers-by. True, the Italians had never filmed the Champs-Élysées or the Place Clichy in this way. It be-came almost obligatory to include in every Nouvelle Vague film one or more long promenades on foot or in a taxi, so that Paris could be discovered 'for the first time'. The new cinema was indubitably fond of a stroll, and shared one quality in common with the tourists one sees in travelogues: the ability to *see* everything without *looking* at anything.

The leaders of the Nouvelle Vague had the avowed desired to appropriate the true talents of the French cinema, so they did a bit of embezzling: 'The Nouvelle Vague was born at Cannes the year that *Hiroshima, Mon Amour, Les Cousins, Orfeu Negro,* and *Les Quatre Cents Coups* were shown,' François Truffaut categorically declared to the journalists of America. All at once, the Press hastened to include in the Nouvelle Vague film-makers who had long pre-ceded it, contradicted it, or had no connection with it at all: I mean Resnais, Varda, Marker, Rouch, Baratier, Gatti, Hanoun, and so on.

Amidst all this carefully built up chaos, what innovations did the Nouvelle Vague really make, apart from introducing new conditions of production and a network of limited but effective mutual aid on the level of public relations ? It would be easier to ask: what innova-tions *could* it have made ? A random re-reading of *Cahiers du Cinéma* is very revealing. That over-estimated magazine, whose chief merit has been to exist longer than its rivals (and publish regularly excellent interviews with directors), has been swamped by three or four successive waves of callow and blustering prophets. Truffaut stated in black and white what a poor opinion he had of Doniol-Valcroze, only to find himself proved wrong one day by some arrogant successor. In the pages of *Cahiers*, the predominant ethos has always been 'make way for me', and this was also the driving force behind the Nouvelle Vague. As generation after generation went its way, the idols were shuffled: those who once worshipped Welles, Huston, and Rossellini were ousted by the champions of Aldrich, Hawks, and Anthony Mann, and then by those of Fuller, Lang, and Losey. Today, all this has been swept away by a new brood of *cinéphiles* who are blithely ignorant of any films that are more than five years old, and new gods have been installed: Ulmer, Walsh, and Cottafavi. The *politique des auteurs* is, as can be seen, a dialectic of hormonal rejuvenation sustained by the criterion of rediscovery on virgin ground. This ability to refocus at will on this or that decade of film history incidentally throws light on another, less obvious, ability: that of denying the true origins of the movement when these origins might be embarrassing. So it is that the Nouvelle Vague officially recognises Melville, Astruc, and Vadim as its involuntary begetters, whereas it displays the greatest contempt for René Clément or Lattuada. And yet one can find the whole of Godard in certain scenes of *The Knave of Hearts* or *Gli Italiani si Voltano* (in *Amore in Città*).

But let us not talk of intellectual rigour. *Cahiers du Cinéma* has, from one generation to another, exalted such perishable goods as *Crin Blanc*, *Si Versailles m'était Conté*, *All About Eve*, *Touchez pas au Grisbi*, *Le Testament d'Orphée*, *L'Ardente Gitane*, or *Le Déjeuner sur l'Herbe*. They have never followed the slightest critical line that one can clearly discern, published the slightest aesthetic manifesto to define common standpoints, elaborated the slightest theoretical system worth taking seriously, apart from an incredibly senile attempt by Rohmer, that Robinson Crusoe of obscurantism.*

---

*See '*Celluloide et Marbre*': 'Can the greatest of painters be so bold as to claim that the face he has painted is truer than the one we see on the screen?' Rohmer, because he wants to prove that the cinema is far

Zazie dans le métro

The *politique des auteurs*, a kind of gimmicky bottle-opener, was always finding that the wine had turned bad: the revelation of Donen at Kelly's expense, the downfall of Aldrich and Ray, the sardonic two-timing of Hitchcock, the unexpected triumph of Antonioni, the decline of Renoir, etc. Cinematic specificity, which allowed Fereydoun Hoveyda to admire Ray's *Party Girl* simply *because* he found the plot particularly silly was held up to ridicule by Richard Roud in *Sight and Sound* ('The French Line', Autumn 1960).

In place of the aesthetic, political, moral, and sociological attitudes of neo-realism, the film-makers from *Cahiers* set up a régime

superior to all other disciplines, camouflages his meaning with a cloak of preciosity and displays a gigantic ignorance of the latest trends in the arts he claims to disparage. It is true that Rohmer is neither a musician like Chaplin, nor a painter like Sirk and Minnelli, nor a poet like Buñuel, nor an architect like Antonioni, nor a man of the theatre like Welles, nor a choreographer like Donen. According to latest reports (of *Le Signe du Lion*) he is no film-maker either. (*Cahiers du Cinéma*, 44.)

of blatant amateurism, of wilful paradoxicality which led them to adopt, through pure whim, certain techniques which the Italians had acquired through necessity. Improvisation which, in Italy, had been an ascetic hardship became for them a sinecure. *A Bout de Souffle* set the fashion for any old thing done in any old way; and although this fashion certainly arose from a deep dissatisfaction with traditional filmic language, it could never raise its convulsions above the level of untidiness. It was, in the full sense of the term, 'rough-draft cinema'.*

Of course, this bias towards glaring negligence was one way of taking the bull by the horns. The Nouvelle Vague is a school of critics who dare each other actually to try their hand at film-making. It is *film-making to see if one is capable of film-making*. It is a mystery how the film-makers of the Nouvelle Vague, in their criticism, have thrown discredit upon John Huston, whom they call an amateur. For the films they produced themselves are amateurish: films in which incompetence, if not the rule, is adopted as a feature of style.

In comparison with everyday, technically over-slick productions, these slapdash films momentarily took the public by surprise – they saw in them, and rightly so, a certain quality of freshness. But it was the freshness of the first attempt; the Nouvelle Vague was important only so long as there were plenty of first attempts. Once incompetence had been overcome (probably reluctantly) and replaced by virtuosity, one pretty quickly noticed in someone like Chabrol an irrevocable decline in sincerity. Once a Nouvelle Vague director learns his profession properly, his breeziness misfires and becomes grotesque. Godard, at the present stage of his career, is no longer creating cinema; moreover, he is trying very hard not to look too much as though he is.

---

*The same dissatisfaction, expressed by that isolated precursor Louis Malle, resulted in *Zazie*, an adult, articulate, and unusually audacious experiment. The seed of ten Nouvelles Vagues is contained in this towering achievement. Malle is an indefatigable searcher, one of those who work for the progress of others; his perpetual dissatisfaction means that his explorations are hazardous, but we are always the richer for them.

For ten years film criticism has had to put up with the lenient annotations of the two great mahatmas of double-talk: Georges Sadoul and André Bazin. And so the last five years have quite naturally been marked by the conviction that it is more worthwhile to make films than to talk about them. The French Cinémathèque was stormed by voracious young men who, to satisfy their secret dream of becoming directors one day, set about wolfing masterpieces by the dozen.

The first result of this was that films were filled with undigested cinema.

There were quotation films, in which such and such a scene from Hitchcock, coupled with another one from Buñuel, leads up to a long Vigo sequence, shot in a Rossellini manner but rejuvenated by Chayefsky techniques. This more or less bulimic assimilation incidentally reflected a real fascination with the act of nutrition. Those who so admired the *pâté de foie* sequence in one of Becker's films lingered long in their own films over breakfasts, snacks, and banquets. But when the act of creation is replaced by the act of consumption, there arises a phenomenon well known in all cannibals: the eater thinks he has invented what he has eaten.*

The cinema, when continually rehashed in this way, inevitably ends up by becoming insipid. The Nouvelle Vague film will give us an imitation, round a bistro table, of some fleeting gesture glimpsed in the third reel of the 1955 remake, in 'Scope, of an old 'B' Western. The height of subtlety consists of making one film in order to say one would like to have made another: 'I would like to dance as they do in Minnelli musicals,' declares Madame Karina, who fails precisely to do so.

The myth of specificity has caused a filmic gold-rush. Paris, already full of young people who possess a painting technique but do not do anything with it, has suddenly found itself invaded by thou-

---

*The first part of *Jules et Jim*, Truffaut's best film, is vitiated by a series of absolutely parasitic private jokes and borrowings which give one the impression of an improvised preamble that has been given a calculated 'Nouvelle Vague look'.

'I would like to dance as they do in Minnelli musicals'. *Une Femme est une Femme*

sands of *cinéphiles* for whom the mere process of direction has taken the place of an act of creation. Their only desire is to make films without even asking themselves what they are going to say in them. By giving the simple fact of self-expression a quotient of value, by substituting the *way* of saying something for any kind of motivation of expression, the champions of the Nouvelle Vague sound as ridiculous as De Gaulle when he reduces his speeches to the formula, so well described by Jean-François Revel: 'You are there, I am here, everything is fine since I am talking to you.' Charles Bitsch's stupid witticism: 'Antonioni has nothing to say and he says it badly' suggests that, in contrast to the latter director, who indissolubly fuses form and content, the Nouvelle Vague is secretly proud of having nothing to say, but of saying it well. This being the case, it is hardly surprising if one has the impression that Godard's films reflect the state of mind of certain manic depressives who spend a lot of time listening to themselves talk without knowing what they are talking about.

Their declared aim is to make great strides forward without worrying too much about an itinerary. And in order to make great strides, the idea is to go as quickly as possible. There is a deceptive creed prevalent among *cinéphiles* which holds that by making many films, of any kind, one will end up one day by finding out what one wants to say, and in that very way one will say it. This delusion is surely just as dangerous as an overlong period as assistant director. In so far as automatic writing cannot be achieved by several people together, there is a fundamental improbability that mere professional activity will strike a creative spark out of a subject. Such an attitude, if not discouraged, would threaten the cinema with an invasion far more catastrophic and depressing than the 'cinema of furnishing'. One might as well build, in great haste and without an architect's plan, a host of houses in the hope that one of them, by some fluke, will be more beautiful than the others.

The Nouvelle Vague has given birth to a mystique of trial and error that enshrines the act of scribbling and glorifies the unfinished. We are supposed to believe that something can be created simply because the author indulges before our very eyes in a bumbling search for a means of expression. It is *Le Mystère Picasso* with, instead of Picasso, someone who is learning to paint. We are supposed to admire the fact that he is learning to paint, and if we remain by his side for a few years we will (perhaps) witness the birth of a painting. Faced with the virtuality of a work that cannot be discussed since it does not yet exist, we are supposed to find the greatest beauty in the greatest flop. Under the pretext of the immediacy of fashion, the highbrow spectator is asked to make out a blank cheque for a future that is all the more promising for remaining distant. It even gets to the point where directors attach a special importance to every slip of speech made by the actors, edit together two versions of the same pout, rave about the chance wobble of the camera, the disastrous shadow of a cloud, the unforeseeable deterioration of the film stock. A Nouvelle Vague film ends up by becoming the resultant of its own shortcomings. And the director ecstatically mucks the whole thing up, in the hope of getting the increasingly admirative derision of the public. If the watchword of neo-realism was: *Facciamo un film; un uomo cerca lavoro* ('Let's make a film; a man looks for work'), that of the Nouvelle Vague might well be: 'I am shooting a film; just look how badly made it is!'

The irony of this is that specificity, which grew from an attempt to make film language autonomous, dooms the latter to systematic deterioration. It encourages a tendency to unmotivated expression, lacking in any deeply felt necessity, and results in a whole string of mannerisms that are destined to die a quick death. The film-makers of the Nouvelle Vague have not caught up with the literature that they so despise. If they devote to the sound-track the assiduous attention they deny their dialogue, it is because they have no roots in the intellectual realities of their time. If they turn their nose up at what they call 'big themes', it is because they are still clinging to the ataxia of pubescent mental defectives, and see themselves threatened by the spectre of culture as though by some omniscient father figure, at once a philosopher and a poet. As far as thought is concerned, their films are thirty years out of date. They are the exact equivalent of those insignificant novels that Gallimard the publishers have been bringing out every year since 1930 just for form's sake, and which the publicity men tart up to make them seem modern.

It should be mentioned at this point that the theory of specificity is influential now only in the field of criticism; the film-makers themselves have long since sacrificed it on the altar of demand. Not only is the Nouvelle Vague now undertaking a fair number of literary adaptations, but it soon gave up the criterion of the 'complete author' which was the rage in 1950 and which, for my part, I continue to uphold. Messrs. Truffaut, Chabrol, and de Broca have set up new teams of scriptwriters, with Moussy, Gégauff, and Boulanger, who have quite simply replaced the old teams, Spaak, Audiard, and Jeanson. Godard, if I am to believe what I read in the newspapers, is adapting his next film from Moravia, as many have done before him. The time when it was a question of all or nothing is past, they are now all doing their little bit in the *film à sketches*, *Les Sept Péchés Capitaux*. One can see that in *Jules et Jim*, François Truffaut has ended up by shooting just the kind of film he would once have attacked: the very principle of a commentary lifted straight from the book (by H.-P. Roché) and read, quite simply, on the sound-track, contradicts all that he was foolish enough one day to write. By this I mean that Truffaut, whose lack of culture has always astonished me, had a lot of luck to come across a good book, to have liked and understood it.

If I keep harping on this idea of specificity, it is because it has acted as a decoy to the young cinema. All cinematographic culture needs to be sublimated, to be confronted with the important ideas of the moment, with the very latest developments in art, science, and poetry. A film is a conflict between rhythm, plasticity, thought, and language. Any film-maker who claims to say something without having a precise idea of what the creative act implies remains a mere technician possessed by a functional frenzy. The cinema cannot be reduced to a syntax of repeatable devices, nor can Cinemascope and the zoom lens play the part of a linguistic manifesto. Bazin was reluctant to analyse anything on the basis of editing, and yet he was not able to convince us of the intrinsic, almost animistic virtues he saw in the sequence shot. The same is true of art, where the use of materials has been unable to alter the major directions of modern painting as practised by Pollock or Arshile Gorky.

The childish mistake of the Nouvelle Vague has been to have made the cinema a god as it was in the time of Dziga Vertov, to have encouraged a professional freemasonry with pretensions to autonomy, and to have attributed to technique the illusory role of an emancipator. Their attitude to literature displays as much old-fashioned isolationism as did William Jennings Bryan before the First World War. They substitute the mirage of narrative *style* for thought and encourage intellectual indifference in young people.

When the indescribable Luc Moullet writes: 'Ethics are a question of tracking shots', it is only to admire 'the gratuitousness, fortunately total, of the camera movements' in the work of Samuel Fuller. The beauty of his tracking shots, if I have understood aright, exempts Fuller from any moral concern, or, better even, authorises him to transcend the world in an orgasm of lateral and circular movements which some see as the very trademark of political uncommittedness. Well, it so happens that every camera movement reveals a movement of thought (an inverse, parallel, or asymptotic movement), even more than the use of the adjective or the third person singular by a writer. The use of violence in film direction, so admired by critics of the extreme right, cannot simply be ascribed to aestheticism, for every style has its moral attitude. Molinaro, who draws his inspiration from one of the most praise-worthy departments of the American cinema, gangster films, cannot help unconsciously inserting, when transposing the techniques of directors like Wise and Aldrich, a morbidity of impact, a taste for physical bruising, a contempt for human fibre, which show him up as the repressed policeman of *Appelez le 17*. Just as Céline's tor-rential sentences betray his anxious fanaticism and his phobia of logical argument, so Fuller's insidious tracking shots contain the hysteria of intellectual rape. 'He has a fine uncouth style,' Moullet sums up admiringly. No, such alibis of exteriorisation simply won't do. What the contemporary French cinema lacks is a philosophic

169

Lola →

Le Farceur

and aesthetic training which could distinguish between creation and mere *mise-en-scène*. The jazz pianist Oscar Peterson, speaking as a teacher of modern music, once declared: 'I don't teach my pupils style, I teach them how to *think*. A musician needs above all to have a sense of direction, and a kind of honesty in his invention.' It is quite obvious that the majority of Nouvelle Vague films are *badly thought out*, except for the more literary among them (*Lola, Le Farceur*, and especially *Paris Nous Appartient*).

The way the film-makers of the Nouvelle Vague shy off the important theme is extremely revealing. They refuse to commit themselves, they escape into formalism. There is, they claim, no subject that cannot be transcended, enlarged, or contradicted by the director. One can make an anti-racialist film with a racialist script, a film for all the family set a few hours before the end of the world, a social film on the falling of a rose petal, a cosmic epic on the passing of the hour at the Greenwich meridian. But it is the moral attitude of the director towards his subject that justifies his role.

L'Année Dernière à Marienbad

Chabrol has said that there are no big themes. He has certainly never plucked up the courage to 'shrink' one, as one shrinks a head; he prefers to magnify microscopic truths. You can fiddle around with the sound-track or the photography, hustle actors and jostle the camera. But certain basic concepts cannot take that kind of treatment.

The Nouvelle Vague's fear of a theme gives itself away by a febrile attempt to amuse. The minute anything important or serious is touched upon, they take refuge in the insipid or the banal. Every point is made by means of gags in the *mise-en-scène*; a sly remark about intellectual treason is treated facetiously. We often get a reassuring wink; we are often informed that none of what is being said is of any consequence. And the mental vacuum is camouflaged by a monologue which makes random mention of a few book titles, or gives a quotation from Gorki which, just for fun, is attributed to Lenin.

At this stage, the argument about content inevitably runs into political considerations. I always mistrust those who display complete indifference to anything in the sphere of ideology. An inquiry in *Cahiers du Cinéma* imagined that the difference between right-wing and left-wing criticism could be removed; it would be done by 'the removal of ethics to the advantage of aesthetics'. I would like to stress that those 'artists', Truffaut and Godard, who, in the name of aesthetics, categorically refuse to be put on either side, agree in their basic credo: 'It amuses me,' says Godard, 'to shuffle the cards.' 'What interests me,' says Truffaut, 'is to contradict myself. . . . I like anything which is confused.' It goes without saying that these are activities that no one denies them. Truffaut, who blamed me in 1956 for ranking him with the young hot-bloods of right-wing criticism, recently gave an interview to *Clarté* which allows us to form a more accurate judgement of his political evolution – which is considerable, as one can judge for oneself: 'A man must vote, but not an artist. He cannot. He ought to try to discover what is interesting in the other man's point of view. . . . There are communist directors in France, and it is they who should be asked to make films about the workers. . . . I refuse to put love at an opposite pole to the *bourgeoisie* or the police. Policemen fall in love too.' Elsewhere, in a outburst of ingenuousness, he admits: 'I knew nothing about politics. I would not have been able to tell you what the FLN was, and then all of a sudden, thanks to TV, I became interested in current affairs.'

This conception of art, which values equivocation and deliberate mystification, this marked taste for everything that blurs one's vision or makes comprehension difficult, represents in all likelihood what Godard, in a brief moment of illumination, put down to a kind of 'right-wing anarchism'. Here is a typical argument: 'In *Le Petit Soldat*, I thought the honest thing was to show friends, I mean people for whom I would go and fight if necessary, and even if I don't exactly *sympathise* with their cause, the Algerians I mean, to show *them* torturing. I thought that torture could be more persuasively condemned if one saw one's own friend practising it.' A remark that does not exactly tally with the following one: 'As I am sentimental, I suppose I am left-wing. Especially compared with my

The torture scene in *Le Petit Soldat*

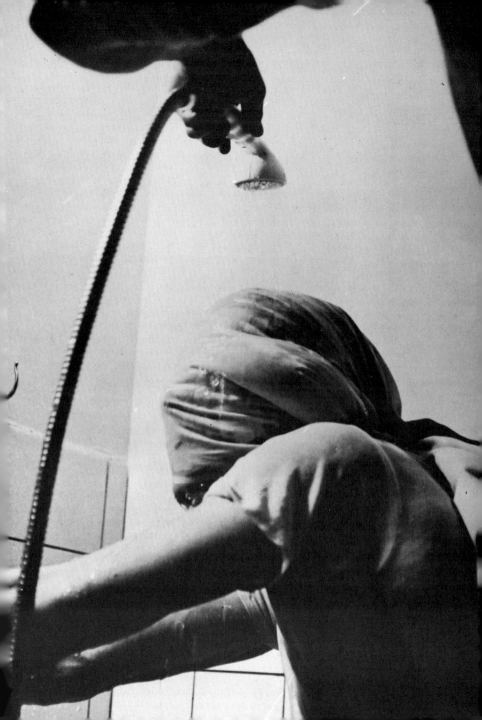

best friends – they are distinctly right-wing.' Here is another quotation in the same vein: 'To me, an artist cannot help being left-wing. Even Drieu La Rochelle was left-wing. Similarly Khrushchev and Kennedy are right-wing, they are totalitarian.' And to conclude: 'On the one hand I am against the police; on the other, I am for them – in the Balzacian sense, in so far as it is mysterious.'

Of course, one has to take into consideration the degree of provocation that informs this faintly preposterous series of statements – their main purpose is to flabbergast the interviewer.* But even when one has done so, one quickly realises that Godard attaches no importance to anything he says. The weight of the spoken word does not worry him, he says anything that comes into his head, just as he films anything that comes into his head, no doubt because 'remorse perhaps results in liberty'. Such self-confidence of course allows him to revere the Establishment, by abstention. Under the guise of anarchy, what we have is a catatonic wait-and-see attitude, a kind of mental hibernation.

Some readers may well have found the thread of this article a trifle sybilline. But I did not impose on myself the rather thankless task of quoting just for fun: I think there is an almost inevitable similarity between the above-quoted remarks and the kind of cinema which they underlie. It is of no great importance to know whether those who made the remarks were unconsciously summing-up their moral conception of aesthetics, or whether, on the contrary, the practice of film-making as an intellectual diversion ensured that sooner or later they would reveal their true political colours. This would involve descending to a personal level; what concerns us here is their films.

And it is here that the Nouvelle Vague's bias in favour of formalism turns against them. As they have no notion of the

---

*I won't quote here the long interview that Godard gave on torture – a disgraceful piece of work. It was however printed, without comment, in the left-wing paper, *L'Express*, which seems to have become Godard's official mouthpiece. And of course each of the gentlemen in question gets his little interview in the right-wing paper, *Clarté*.

elementary processes of the unconscious in artistic creation, they think themselves rid of all that they repress, and adduce a lack of interest in politics which is contradicted by their continual defiance when they deny their bias. However, their epigoni are less cautious: 'Fascism is beautiful,' declares Luc Moullet, who writes a little later: 'The only opinion of Fascism that is worthy of consideration is that of somebody who has been tempted by it.' Marc C. Bernard, who considers that 'every historical subject should be conceived and treated as though it were the subject of a gangster film', states that 'brutality is one way of doing things, and an honest one too'. It goes without saying, as his mentor Michel Mourlet points out, that only 'brutality of expression and of photography' is meant by this. We had got the distinction. Michel Mourlet, in an article entitled 'In Defence of Violence', explained it well: 'The work of Walsh is an illustration of Zarathustra's aphorism: "Man is made for war, woman for the warrior's rest, and the rest is folly".' We can find in these wild admirers of Jacques Laurent, 'the writer who has written the finest and frankest sentences about girls' muscles' (Marc C. Bernard), the traditional aesthetic alibis of the extreme right and the cowardice of all those who admire and adore gangsterish ideas and brutal language, while at the same time shrilly denying their inevitable context.

To put it bluntly, this is the kind of furtive hide-and-seek that eventually reveals the most treacherous characteristics of right-wing thinking. There are not many intellectuals nowadays who avouch reactionary ideology. But the subtle talkers who are deaf to their own words, the over-zealous champions of form as opposed to content, and the passionate devotees of mental chaos – i.e. the freedom to say anything that comes into their head – all unfailingly reveal a nostalgia for arbitrary power.

And so the argument about content is to me the chemical element which *precipitates* the environment and separates the molecules. Contrary to what one might expect, defining left-wing cinema in relation to right-wing cinema is not the same thing as gauging a work's degree of political effectiveness. On the contrary, I think the left-wing cinema can be defined by its faults. An unsuccessful left-wing film is always overweighted in content, it is often awkward-ly sincere, and it covers too many problems at once because it is too keen to convince. It tends to be too explicit and to simplify the forms of exposition. To go from there and exhort left-wing film-makers to include more deliberate indifference, carelessness, and blurred impressionism on the pretext that they are in fashion would be absurd. On the other hand, one might ask them to have recourse more frequently to Hegelian dialectic, to give themselves more distance from their subject, to use analogy more frequently, to be more unbridled in their lyricism, and to employ a technique of surprise which would counter the current tenets of sloth; these are all qualities that one finds in directors such as Valerio Zurlini, Alexander Singer, and Alain Cavalier.

Positif is now at what might be called a turning-point in its existence. It will attempt *to rid the French cinema of bourgeois ideas*. The Nouvelle Vague, compared with other post-war movements in the cinema, represents a palliative regression, a misuse of analytical and critical activities which tends to limit or discredit the real attempts at renewal which film language is undergoing; the real contribution of these attempts will be assessed by *Positif* and will be compared with that of the Nouvelle Vague. Our aim in demolishing these *bourgeois* attitudes is above all to attack excessive chauvinism. What is happening every day in Poland and Italy, what is still happening in the prodigious melting-pots of America pours ridicule on the dilatory experiments of our playboys. We shall stand up for the principle of internationalism, which destroys outdated concepts of schools and throws into relief the significant and constant values of the moment.

What we write will be aimed in particular at the younger genera-tion. They have been conditioned by the Algerian War, and their frequently brutal collision with political and social realities means that they are hardly likely to find sustenance in the deification of technique or in the demagogy of form which results in bread being replaced by its image, the image by its reflection, and the word by its echo.

The normal process of professional training (film school, assistantship) should not necessarily be championed in place of the dilettante formulae of the Nouvelle Vague. The future surely lies in the hands of a generation of film-makers who are above all preoccupied with their own ideological emancipation and are already making, as best they can, militant films that bear witness to modern society – and on the side are learning how to use a camera. This generation is using its ingenuity not to devise systems of self-publicity, but to overcome, in the secrecy that circumstances demand, the material difficulties that their convictions impose upon them.

We shall treat the cinema as *one* of several means of expression, neither inferior nor superior to the others, and we shall submit films to criteria which do not subordinate moral and sociological considerations to aesthetic ones. We shall be careful not to confuse the mere practice of a profession with the creative act, or communal activity with the elaboration of a work of art. We shall ask that film-makers be allowed to mature their works, instead of being forced to make slapdash jobs simply because the industry demands two films a year from them. We shall allocate to each film as much time as is needed for any important work, literary or philosophical, to be generated. We shall not indulge in the unbelievable glibness of talking about the cinema solely in technical terms, we shall refuse to set any limit on our imagination, and we shall subject films to all kinds of analogy. We shall base our appreciation of cinema on the identification of the intellectual content with its external envelope, and we shall make a sharp distinction between personal style and the mannerisms of the day. We shall go back to the fundamental idea of a 'personal universe' that was established by the review *L'Age du Cinéma*. We shall answer any attempts to confuse by applying unruffled analysis which, while completely impervious to notions of fashion, will not exclude the wildest interpretations.

It goes without saying that such a standpoint is situated at opposite poles to the ideal of *improvised cinema*. If it still holds that 'true art cannot help being revolutionary', we shall always refuse to put a limit on the number of themes or subjects that it may be permitted to treat. We are here in full agreement with the manifesto that André Breton and Leon Trotsky drew up in 1938, *For Inde-pendent Revolutionary Art*, the terms of which remain indisputable: 'To those who try to persuade us that art should be subjected to a discipline which we consider to be radically incompatible with its means, our refusal will be categorical. It is our deliberate will to keep to the formula: *any licence in art.* . . . In defending freedom of creation, we intend in no way to justify political indifference. It is far from our purpose to wish to resuscitate the concept of so-called 'pure' art, which usually serves the far from pure aims of reactionary ideas. . . . It is more worth while to trust in the gift of prefiguration which is the prerogative of every authentic artist, which implies the beginning of a (virtual) solution to the most serious contradictions of his age and orientates the thinking of his contemporaries towards the urgent need to establish a new order.'

Bibliography

Barthes, Roland: interview with, in *Cahiers du Cinéma* 147.

Bazin, André: *What is Cinema?* University of California Press, Berkeley and Los Angeles 1967. Essays by André Bazin, selected and translated by Hugh Gray, from *Qu'est-ce que le Cinéma?*, originally published in four volumes by Editions du Cerf (Septième Art), Paris 1958–62.

Bazin, André; and Cocteau, Jean: *Orson Welles*. Chavane, Paris 1950.

Benayoun, Robert: *La nébuleuse de l'épate-bourgeois* (review of *Alphaville*), in *Positif* 71.

Benayoun, Robert: *La machine à décerveler* (review of *Pierrot le Fou*), in *Positif* 73.

Borde, Raymond: *Cinéma français d'aujourd'hui* in *Nouvelle Vague*. SERDOC (Premier Plan, no. 9), Lyons 1962.

Brémond, Claude; Sullerot, Evelyne; and Berton, Simone: *Les héros des films dits 'de la Nouvelle Vague'* in *Communications* I. Editions du Seuil.

Cahiers du Cinéma:
    71: *Table ronde sur le Cinéma Français.*
    91: Special issue in memory of André Bazin.
    126: Special issue on criticism.
    138: Special issue on the *Nouvelle Vague.*
    150–151: Special issue on American cinema.

Cinéma 60: Aujourd'hui la Nouvelle Vague, in nos. 42, 43, 44.

Curtelin, Jean: *Marée Montante* in *Nouvelle Vague*. SERDOC (Premier Plan, no. 10), Lyons 1962.

Durgnat, Raymond: *Nouvelle Vague, the first decade*. A Motion Monograph. Motion Publications, London 1963.

Godard, Jean-Luc: *Bergmanorama*, in *Cahiers du Cinéma* 85. Also, in *Cahiers du Cinéma in English* no. 1.

Godard, Jean-Luc: *Des larmes et de la vitesse* (review of *A Time to Love and a Time to Die*) in *Cahiers du Cinéma* 94.

Godard, Jean-Luc: *Feu sur Les Carabiniers* (answers to criticisms of film), in *Cahiers du Cinéma* 146.

Hoveyda, Fereydoun: *La réponse de Nicholas Ray*, in *Cahiers du Cinéma* 107.

Kyrou, Ado (one of the editors of *Positif*): *Luis Buñuel: An Introduction*. Simon and Schuster, New York 1963. Originally published by Editions Seghers (*Cinéma d'aujourd'hui*, no. 4) Paris 1962.

Labarthe, André S.: *Essai sur le jeune cinéma français*. Le Terrain Vague, Paris 1960.

Legrand, Gérard: *Le Mépris*, in *Positif* 59.

Morin, Edgar: *Conditions d'apparition de la 'Nouvelle Vague'*, in *Communications* I. Editions du Seuil.

Moullet, Luc: *Jean-Luc Godard*, in *Cahiers du Cinéma* 106.

Mourlet, Michel: *Apologie de la violence*, in *Cahiers du Cinéma* 107.

Pilard, Philippe: *Nouvelle Vague et politique*, in *Image et Son* 188.

Positif:
   31: *Quoi de neuf?* (discussion on *Nouvelle Vague*).
   36: *Enquête sur la critique.*
   46: *Feux sur le cinéma français* (special issue on *Nouvelle Vague*).
   64–65: *Aspects du cinéma américain.*

Rivette, Jacques: *De l'abjection* (review of *Kapo*) in *Cahiers du Cinéma* 120.

François Truffaut making *Fahrenheit 451*.

Rohmer, Eric; and Chabrol, Claude: *Hitchcock*. Editions Universitaires, Paris 1957.

Rohmer, Eric: *Le goût de la beauté*, in *Cahiers du Cinéma* 121.

Thirard, Paul-Louis: *Paris Nous Appartient* in *Positif* 35.

Truffaut, François. *Hitchcock*. Simon and Schuster, New York 1967; to be published in Autumn 1968 by Secker and Warburg, London. Originally published as *Le Cinéma Selon Hitchcock* by Robert Laffont, Paris 1966.

Truffaut, François: *Positif copie zéro*, in *Cahiers du Cinéma* 79.

A full bibliography of Alexandre Astruc is to be found in *Alexandre Astruc* by Raymond Bellour. Editions Seghers (*Cinéma d'aujourd'hui* no. 10), Paris 1963.

A full bibliography of Jean-Luc Godard is to be found in *The Films of Jean-Luc Godard*, edited by Ian Cameron. A Movie Paperback, Studio Vista, London 1967.